Tha Miracle Bout Uh' Hustler

Poetry book
By.
Joseph Flowers
The Govenor

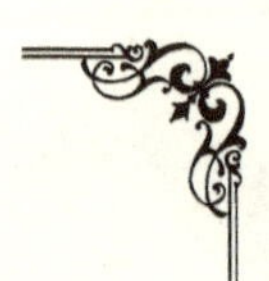

Published by exclusively House Reps Publishing
First edition Love Got Eyes

ISBN: 979-8-9880934-3-5

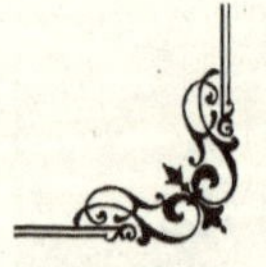

ABOUT THE AUTHOR

Greetings
It's my pleasure you have offered spending the time letting me bring you into my world. Upon you finish I would be very honored if you had the time reviewing the book thereof. Although, if you're to busy that's well. You might only decide leaving the stars. Either way I would love to acknowledge your perceptions for improving my craft in the books to follow.

Also if you like to reach me or get the latest updates of any new materials whether music or books / visit my website: Books of bulk orders available:
Www.Houserepspublishing.com
Social media outreach:
Instagram @thegove.s.o
Facebook: Joseph Gov Flowers
https://linktr.ee/theGove.s.o
https://youtube.com/@thegovenor
Looking forward to interactions with my readers. Thanks much!

CONTENTS

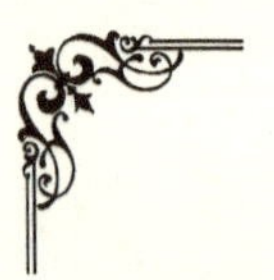

ACKNOWLEDGMENTS

My deepest thoughts I forward to those who stayed mindful, hopeful and optimistic of my journey as a poet, writer and author. The strength you have provided is unmatched too many to list. If you have any questions- you're the reasons im motivated to get lost in these thoughts daily. My Grandparents rest in power of both sides, Moms & Pops, my Sisters, Brothers, Uncles, Aunties, Neices, Nephew's and Cousins in drowds. Those who've received their wings before the hours upon my absence; love you- miss you more than words could ever express!

A genuine thanks for the efficient utmost support throughout the years my House Reps worldwide, Urbanlife & Rapbay Distribution, can't forget the hustlin' homey's around the globe- there are No Limits! The hood I grew up and learnt the lifestyles of uh' hustler.

Best friend "B" you're always that some-one whom gives me hope. Thanks forever, proud of you!

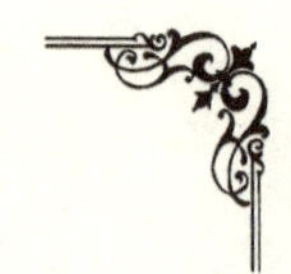

Original Cupid's Innocence

Just of admiring outta dynamics
Identical stares unspoken for
Vaguely said aside how's it tightwad fit
Often fighting back within our glares
Impatiently pasting I'm over-intrigued
Not resistance declare our innocence
We're spray paint's blush
Imbedded views courage won't reveal
Say now should our innocence hold a grudge
Cause words like hearts forever need trust
Original upset how you sway whatz "us"
If eyes couldn't speak
Effects wouldn't blush

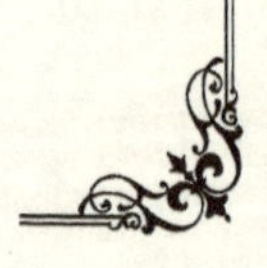

These somewhat my thoughts I endured while up against the battles over my life—positioned where anything I hoped to questioned, others found the tendencies to oppose, irrespective having known their insights were based on sets of prejudgmental conclusions. Yet, I channeled my anger in prayer and boldly did not let my most brittle opinions get the best of me. Thereof my pursuits of relief politely spoke within. I conversated right alone and silently; letting the answers I'd yearned of approach my viable solutions. A suspense of uncertainties lead me, but I unshiftingly followed a tender knock that now holds an amplifying disposition of my life's profound innocence.

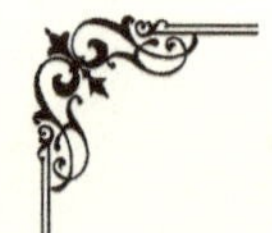
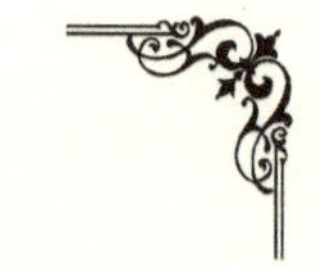

Should I Answer That

Nothing speaks louder than verbs
How did that slip away
That non-exculpatory vacate
Imaginations aren't understated languages
Maybe we oughta listen these lifetime
Some things takes awhile
Luck happens to work ingeniously
Pay attention it's getting kinda interesting
Why don't we, or I have competition
Okay you not listening
Ordering inside those thoughts
Those butterflyz zoned on their own?
I wished I could spurce dat aloud
Haven't you peeped out what's ours rebound

We're brighter if bundled in self-wisdom
Inference has to bezel consistence
Spread your beautiful stark faintest thoughts
If hearts hadn't marched
Our souls wouldn't kick start

A modern-day world in forward
Only thing we oughta have to fear
Is fear itself
Deeply rooted historic we dealt

The realz hon'
I bangz cowbells
If our fears were of hell- drops
We'd vanished in puddles of tearz
Instead of insecurities we've aboard
Halmark varieties placing our nation first
For pivotal inferences hearts truly record

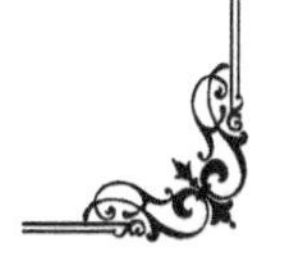

"Should 👁 Answer that"

Nothing speaks louder than verbs
How did that slip away
That exculpatory chance visit
Imaginations aren't understated languages
Maybe we oughta listen These lifetime

Somethings takes awhile
Luck happens to work ingenuously
pay attention its getting kinda intresting
why dont we, or I have competition
Okay you not listing
Ordering inside Those Thoughts
Those butterflyz zoned on their own ?
I wished I could sparce dat out

Havent you peeped out what's ours rebound
We're brighter bundled in self wisdom
Infferance has to bezel consistance
Spread your beautiful stark faintest thoughts
if hearts hadn't marched
Our souls wouldn't kick start
A modern day world in forward
Only thing we oughta have to fear
Is fear itself
Deeply rooted historic we dealt

The realz hon
I bangz Cowbells
If our fears were of helldrops
We'd vanished in puddles of tearz

AJ.

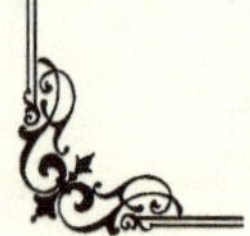
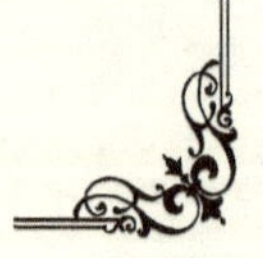

Instead of insecurities we've aboard
Halmark varities placing our nation first
For pivotal inferances hearts truly record !!.

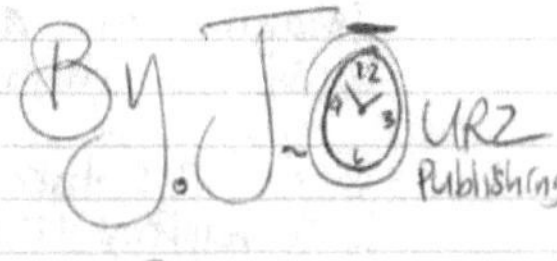

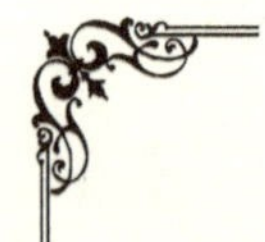
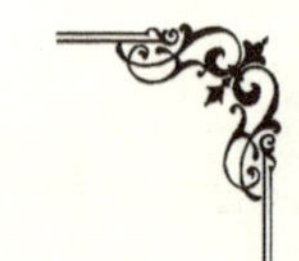

Confidence Attaches Reflections

Baptized off my alarm
Those who are bracing looking for the reciprocal
I'm holding my tongue
Adoring my knocks
You to superstitions
Constitutions of the Fourteenth Amendments

Who said not real huggz
They gotta be igloos
By insinuations you to rhetorical
It's not going to be over until
That's beyond a concealed signal
"Unidentified"
Almost routinely nearly inaudible still

Yet I'm immutably frostbitten
Whose whispers keep breathing
Consensus beauties of yourz
Hard to diminish
Our life's uh' journey I've learnt
Like you I listened never lost sight of the bounce

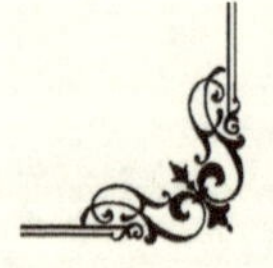

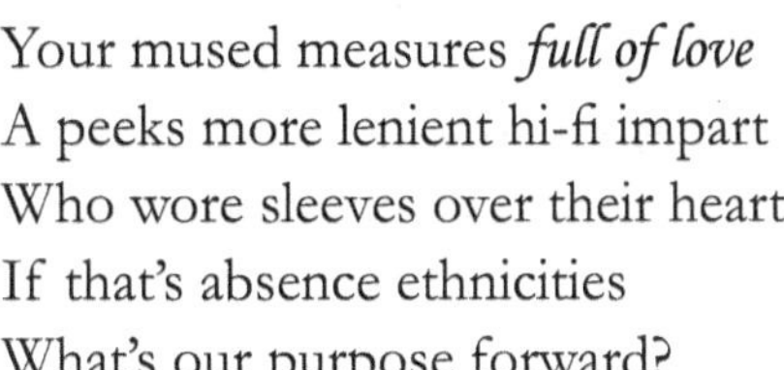

Your mused measures *full of love*
A peeks more lenient hi-fi impart
Who wore sleeves over their heart
If that's absence ethnicities
What's our purpose forward?

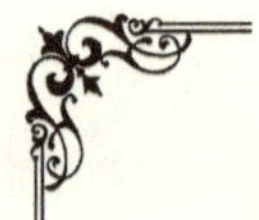
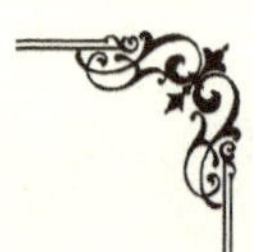

After managing between dialogues while perceiving of something of value of yours under observant pairs of wondering eyes at a thousand miles per second apart, but insynce at heart it was almost impossible of ignoring her bite – which grew louder than uncaged minds ready for a change. Authentic love sometimes come heaven sent, reasons I wrote about these thoughts and to share these leaps of.. inspired likely matching of identical persistence. "She knows the dial." Imagine what's on my mind.

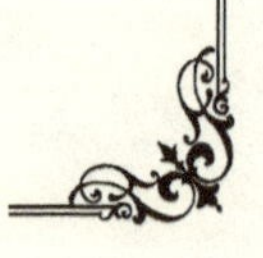

Off The Dribble

Beyond the visibles of life
The finer things above that bounce
Those thoughts from court sides
Brights that shoned
Popping out the wits
Despite the lights timid
Visuals of impressive peaks
Voices from boundaries of the free
You wondering which zones of prominently
Strikes at the heart of Batson Wheeler beliefs
The spirit-the-waif
That's not such biases impacts
I'm done shadow boxing
Let's endure our moments submerged
While conversing with one another
Humans yearn those basic instincts
It's laughable to begin the synonymous "if"
Intentional or mistake Kentucky's guidances
The equal rights upon every U.S. citizen
We've reached the hype of the burgs
Yourz agree?

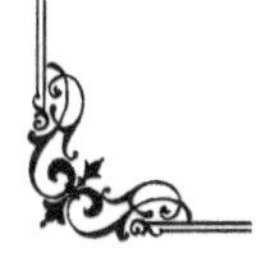

"OFF th Dribble"

Beyond the visibles of life
The finer things above that bounce
Those thoughts from Court Sides
Brights that Shoned
Popping out the wits
Despite the lights timid
Visuals of impressive Peaks
Voices from boundaries of the free
You wondering which zones of prominently
Strikes the heart of Baston Wheeler beliefs
The Spirit-the-waif
That's not such biases impacts
I'm done Shadow boxing
Let's endure our moment Submerged
While conversing with one anther
Humans yearn those basic instincts
It's laughable to begin the synonymous "IF"
Intentional or mistake Kentucky's guidances
The equal rights upon every U.S Citizen
We've reached the hype of the burgs
Yourz agree?

By. J Ourz
Publishing
©2024

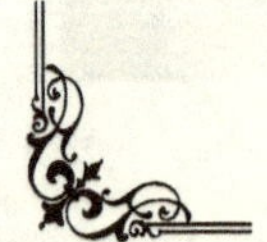

HER LOVE GOT EYES

So deep swagger to spare
Who's dial mine or yourz
Maybe the runways to dared
I'm untangled myself let's be bold
Speak what's on your mind love~
Beneficial we pursue upon fleet
A leap of instincts
You said no compromise fine
Despite the weather or New Jersey tides
No running in place, but caged our fears
Like trap-n-space
Focused with expectations nondistorted
On speed bound inescapable now
The things you desired I forgot ourz
Promise induce furious eyes
Don't gotta hide yourself
Redial who's woken now
Not a sound uncraved
US Olympians residue unmisbehaved
Strengths include geometry traits
If I could quest "love"
How you vamp my gaze?

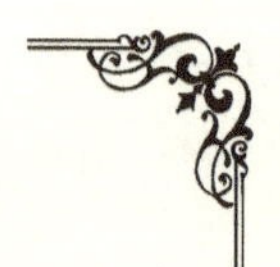

I've designed this for a tender heart often maneuvered between the waves, you knew we were destined, but somehow got tangled up during the desired things humans does – exploring life without worries. Yet appears the world was present, listening or I mighta misjudged. But I appreciate her brave, courageous, unspeakable ways; although simile have danced and held her, but only momentarily. This I write for her conformation. "Love's real– beyond those glitters and glams." It was my pleasure learning your moves. I've watched you; you've provided a mental balance though more than just words, unlike others before you– you were always there, attentive, present and never missed a beep. No, I wasn't ignoring you, in fact, I heard you loud-n-clear. It's almost unfair how you be tossing money by stares. That Ms. Tenderly~Mc. January thing you have underneath; I happen only seen just enough that reinforces how the spirit works, as they say beauty doesn't have reasons to limit itself. It's proven, you may believe farther than

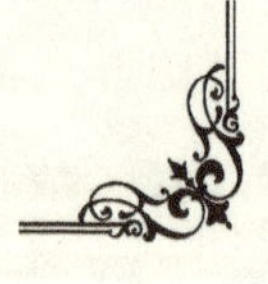

sight and the six of senses, you need to not speculate the leaner it'll define the outter layers before you know it. Until, please don't let the deep and dark state with murky – polluted cloudy debris out their steal your compassion, determination nor quest for happiness. Stay humble, peaceful yet mindful. "Love conquers hate."

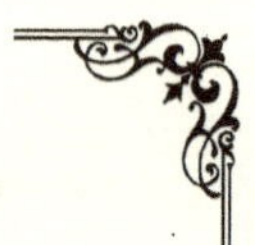

"Her Love Got Eyes"

So deep swagger to spare
Who's dial mine or yourz
Maybe the runways to dared
I'm untangled myself lets be bold
Speak whats on your mind love
Benefical we pursue upon fleet
A leap of instincts
You said no compromise fine
Despite the wheather or New Jersey tides
No running in place, But 👁 caged our fearz
Like trap-N-space

Focused with expectations non distorted
On speed bound inescapable now
The things you desired I forgot ourz
promise induce furious eyes recognize
Don't gotta hide yourself
Redial who's woken now
Not a sound uncraved
U.S Olypians residue unmisbehaved
Strenghts include geometry traits
If I could quest "Love"
How you vamp my gaze?

By Jourz
Publishing

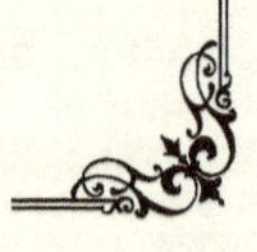

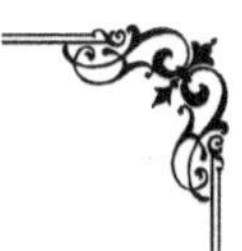

I've designed this for a tender love often maneuvered between the waves, you know we were destined, But somehow get tangled up durning the desired Things humans does— exploring life without worries; yet appears the world was present, listining or I mighta missed Judged. But I appriciate her brave-courageous unspeakable ways; although simile have danced and held her, but only momentarily. This I write for her comformation. "Love's real— beyond Those glitters and glams". It was my pleasure learning your moves. I've watched you, you've provided a mental blance through more than Just words, unlike others before you— you were always there, attentive, present and never missed a beep. No; I wasn't ignoring you; infact; I heard you loud-N-Clear. It's almost unfair how you be tossing rock stars by stares. That Ms. Tender Mc. January thing you have underneath; I happen only seen Just enough that reinforces how the spirit works; As they say beauty doesn't have reasons to limit itself; it's Proven, you may believe farther than sight and the six of senses, you need to not speculate the leaner it'll define the outter layers before you know it. until, please dont let the deep and dark state with murky-polluted cloudy debris out their steal your compassion, determination nor quest for happness. Stay humble, peaceful yet mindful. "Love" conquires hate!

Sea Taste

Taste gravity under tears quotes
Yet they're very inspiring
Alarming I'm forewarned
Taste dreamy and exotic
Visible worthy for prints
Reasons they insured
Taste like opportunity surrounds us
Genuine what's unrecorded
Huh, taste
Braver imaginations our quite
Solitude confined made "us" jealous
Taste the secrets of multiple wishes
Flooded in diamonds
Homey stocks day ripe

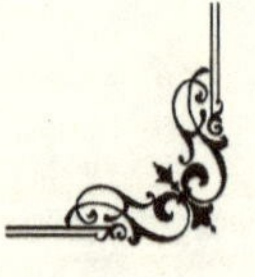

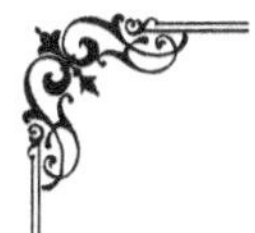

Noticed something of the sexiest on the globe's planet earth from another perspectives "dialed," taste was a place of scale and mind, which came during the analyzing of this beauty that's deserving of runway lustful praises, hadn't hurt the off the hinges—fetchings of her irresistible smiles, but something about her position of quest and beauty she exercised the hell outta my sight and mind—now the decisions I make are reflective of her yelling, but silent, imaginations. "If only you knew!" But it's for only the "unobvious" my responses I'll contain, still holding my heels to the grain, as I admire her from distance's utilizing cautions—not to uneven the stares, which often utters outta nowhere on their own ways; in particular; yet sparking and revealing [whether via-photographed impressed] her beauty it's a mental gymnastic optical, I'll have to learn suppressing those shots. Do I desire? Thus, my initial comment would be, "Never hurts to ask." It's the Oracle bites of my good mornings, daily my taste for the blurred lines of our disparities brings out the tucked love scruti-

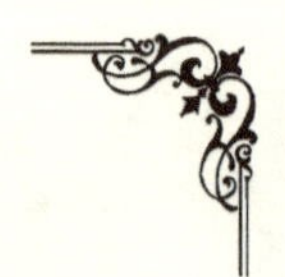

ny from the have-nots. Yet; I as her, am mindful more aware likely than not. The nation isn't of prepared not even close for how well she wears faithfully that signature prance, for it's only fit for uh' king, and that bounce—she's daring! What a powerful force to be reckoned with—it's kinda that fabric you'd not often hesitate for imposing a knee to the gravel. I wonder knot I could stomach to negotiate ways without-um, taste.

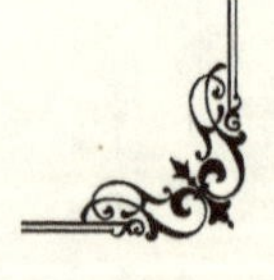

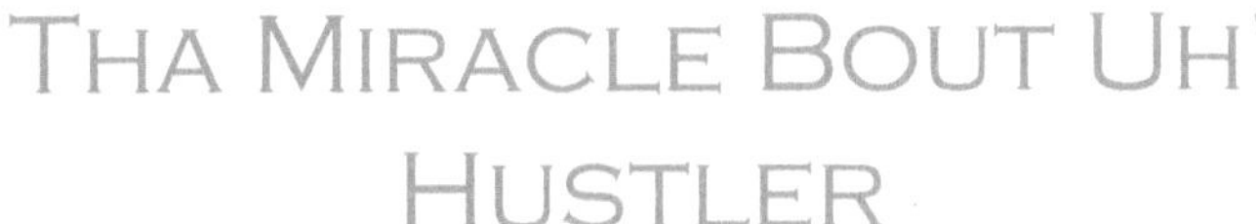

THA MIRACLE BOUT UH' HUSTLER

Standby ready
Not that we have to flex
It's room for any adjustabilities
Mindful of setbacks "yet"
Playing fields level
Whispered between "us"
I'm adventurous despite staying on course
Unapologetic our status quo
Well-schooled too headstrong

Desires now more than ever
Sparks flew raised every eyebrow who?
Black slide on razor blades without getting blusters
Farewell controversial
I overstood what you meant
Imaginations react
The spotlights bright you meeting me?

Uncompromised those watery eyes
First time hold next time swipe right
Stay ready beyond insight our methods on pace

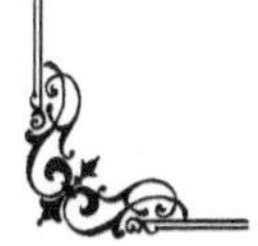

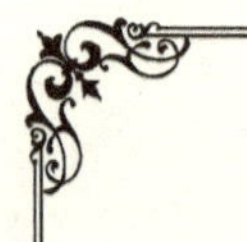

Brighter by the day
Peek cream gotta taste

Bona fide bidder beyond judgmental
Breathable playbook
In rhythm hers I'm obsessed wit "um"
Luxuries appetite combined
Equivalent where love lives
Front stage pivotals you surprised by vintages
I'm adlibbing mine's no sonic
Try'n ta expand that gap
How we define the sign of the times
Often unexpressed but phenomenal as art
Not a mystery so wishful
Only for you though just letting you know
"Tha Miracle Bout Uh' Hustler"

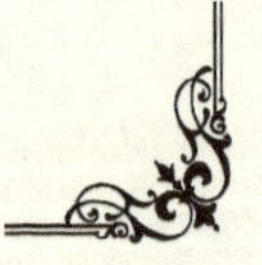

These were a part of some of my roughest weathers where nothing I done propelled against the hurdles that sorta indented upon me. Whether on flukes and or purposeful, school test or the needs reachin' family and or friends, the outer world was at distances. I likewise was maintaining my focus not hurting those of within closest. Although the ups 'n downs had its days. But the happiness of hers appeared to depend upon whether I achieved, and plenty instances from unpreventable, physical strains coupled had I hadn't noticed. Yet my hardest & roughest tucked fears of not scoring.. was obvious from the actions that surrounded us daily. Still internalized I overcame, and the smile that gazed those features lit up the world around the globe—and beyond our wishes. (I doubt she knew) I continue with prayer and in absence of bail persistence plus- faith is always the right traits.

"Tha Miracle Bout Uh' Hustler"

"THA MIRACLE BOUT UH' HUSTLER"

Standby ready
Not That we gotta flex
It's room for any adjustibilities
Mindful of set backs
Playing fields level
whispers between "us"
I'm adventurous despite staying on course
Unpologetic our status quo
Well schooled too head strong

Desires now more than ever
sparks flew raised every eye brow who?
Back slide on razor blades without getting blusters
Fare well controversal
I overstood what you ment
Imaginations react the spot lights bright
You meeting me?

Uncompromused those watery eyes
First time hold
Next time swipe right
Stay ready beyond insight
Our methods on pace
Brighter by the day
peek cream gotta tast?

Bona fide bidder beyond judgmental
Breathable playbook
In rhythm "I'm obsessed with 'um'
Luxuries appetite combined
Equivalent where love lives

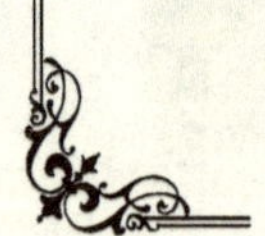
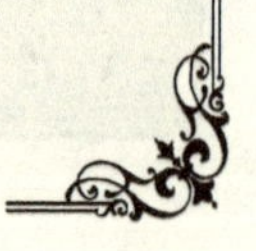

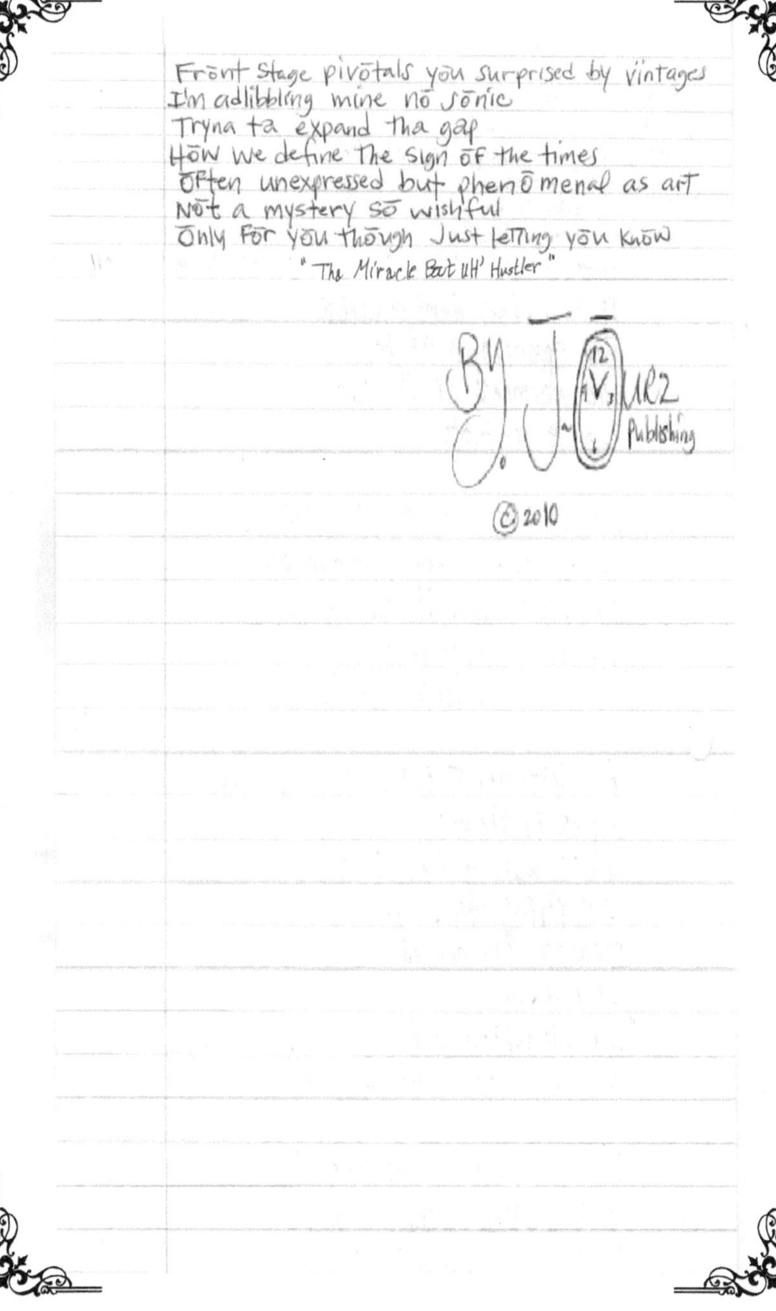

Front Stage pivotals you surprised by vintages
I'm adlibbing mine no sonic
Tryna ta expand tha gap
How we define The sign of the times
Often unexpressed but phenomenal as art
Not a mystery so wishful
Only For you though Just letting you know

"The Miracle But UH' Hustler"

By

Publishing

© 2010

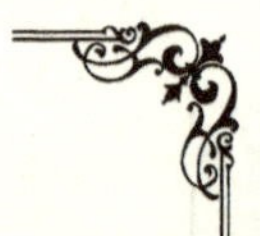

These were apart of some of my roughest times
where nothing I done propelled against the hurdles
that sorta indented upon me. Whether on uh' fluke,
School test or the reachin family and or friends - the
the outter world was of importance and maintaining
my focus, not hurting those very closest durning the
ups and downs, her happness appeared to depend upon
whether I achived, and plenty days I hadn't from
unpreventable physical strains, yet my hardest
brought out hidden tears, which was obvious from
the actions of mines. That hurted, but im internalized
I overcame and the smile that gazed those features
lit-up the world around the globe - beyond our
wishes. (I doubt she knew) I continue with prayer
and in absence of bail, gravity meets. Goes to
show, presistance "plus" faith is always the right
traits.

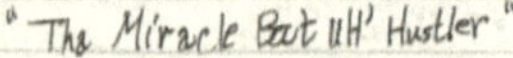

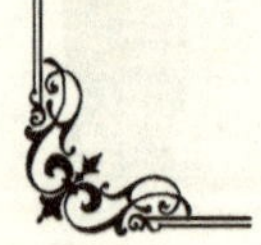
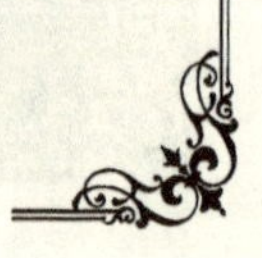

Significant's Value

Ridding for us our days are essential
Endure with variety speculating
Even though there is a variance
The values held are sentiment
With a mutual understanding
Suited ready with natural reflexes
Without slightest hesitations
Who wouldn't notice checkmate
Substain as the world awaits
"*No pressure*"
Sensitive to light like films focused within
I asked lake forest rims
Who's we confused how forever bells pitched

Initiative beyond shore bait
Despite American's opinion
I'm determined by implied world existence
Unlike the war on poverty's vision vivid
I'm not angry boasting veer
Just analyzing see forgiveness for *ocean ring tones*

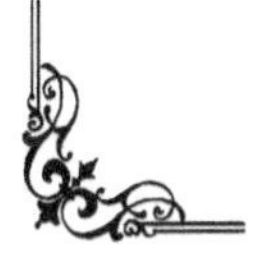

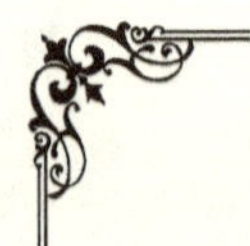

Those almost deviated of hope
Every roads marched on
Every breath counted for
No eyes unnoticed batlike
Farther than imaginary which makes humans
Human beings
Say hi lake forest distinguish way in

Same ol' love
Gladly bursted outta tearz
For particular purposes let's include yourself
Yup amnesty you're too invited
Cost is waived
Adventures on the house
Let our foresights be brave
This no peace bail bench warrants
A legend observed those rangs
Not to discovery clarity
Bet volume the world's raised

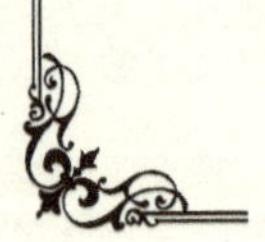
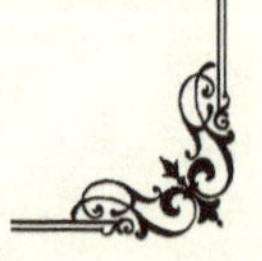

The value of tha inkling of these thoughts how someone's willing of putting on the table their life for a primary purpose of auther's vision—with me comes full surface and holds an ultimate unilluminated prospects any person could wish for. It's in my opinion equivalent of an inspiring heart held spouse, ride or die contentions, as those notions are notable powerful, refreshing and heartwarming with me particularly~ because while writing in my journal those thoughts I myself was absent this lucky some tinted lover—whom I believed our uniting glows in honesty were further than imaginary. Although the two of us hadn't never meet in the florals of physical form, but I based our foundation and relations on implied existences, like photographs, friends of persons we likely may have known or not quit—but through the values God promises. Ask and likely you'll receive {the least} options; from the optimistic focal which was prayed for and sealed with a kiss of her mannerist kind. Fun part about it; our bound shared, "it's perfectly spaced," considering any virtue aspects. I'll quit it goes deeper like the Napoleon theory.

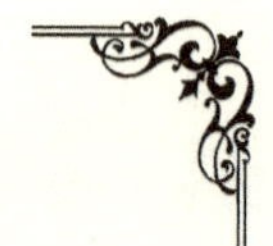

"Significant's Valu~~~"

Ridding for us our days are essential
Endured with variety speculating
Even though they're are variances
The Values held are sentiment
with a mutual understanding
Suited ready with natural reflexes

without slightest hesitations
who wouldn't notice checkmate
Substain as the world awaits
"No preasure"
Sensitive to light like films focused within
I asked Lake Forest rims
who's we confused how forever bells pitched

Initative beyond shore bait
I'm determined by implied world existence
unlike the warz on poverty's vision Vivid
I'm not angry boasting Veer
Just analizing see forgiveness for Ocean ringtones
Those almost deviated of hope

Every roads marched on
Every breathe counted for
No eyes unnoticed bat like
Farther than imagainary
which makes humans humanly beings
Say hi Lake Forest distinguish way in

Same ol' love
Gladly bursted outta tearz

FOR Particular Purposes include yourself yup
Ammesty your invited
Cost is waived
Adventures on the house
Let our foresights be brave

This no peace bail bench warrants
A legend observed those rangs
Not to discover clarlty
"Bet value the worlds raised"

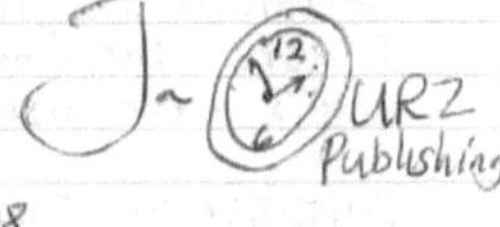

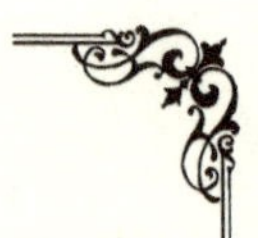

The value of the inkling of the thoughts how someone's willing of putting on the table their life for a primary purpose of anthers vision — with me comes full surface and holds an ultimate unilluminated prospects any person could wish for. It's in my opinion equlavant of an inspired heart held spouse, ride or die contentions, as those notions are notable powerful, refreshing and heart warming. with me particularly because while writting in my journel those thoughts; I myself was absent this luckly some tinted lover- whom I believed our uniting glows in honesty were further than imagainary; Although; the two of us hadn't never meet in the florals of physical form; but I based our foundation and relations on implied existences, like photographs friends of persons we likely may have known or not quit — but through the values god promises. Ask and likely you'll recive [the least] options; from the optimistic focial which was prayed for and sealed with a kiss of her mannerist kind. Fun part about it; our bound shared; "It's perfectly spaced", considering any virtue aspects; I'll quit it goes deeper like the Napōleōn theory.

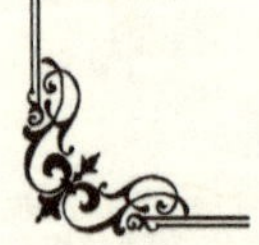
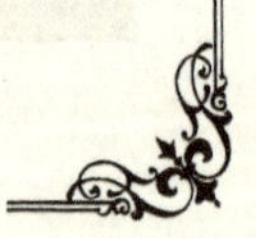

Her Exotic Aroma

Her bite of sunshine's "ham"
Gravity meets the eyes
What others tend to ignore
She finds to magnifies
Commands attention hardly not trying
She hugs her hips incidently
Teases her own eyelids
I would love too
But she tripple blinded kindly
Thinking of her *exotic aroma*
I'm wishful fully enriched
Off the whiff
Possibly she's more than hazardous
Than I'm able to read
I pray conditions were different
Our two realities warrants game changes
What ah' strange pleasure
Her *exotic aroma*
It's potent ain't it
How it flows through my visuals

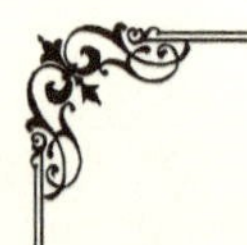

Polarizes my untamed obsessions
Imagine a better distraction
To begin it merits
Lies claustrophobics of a sleeping giant
Wow I believe
Just as does plenty
Missed the lessons how to show affection?
Rebounds equals hope
Am I asking the world
        Evoking a half ah' cenote?

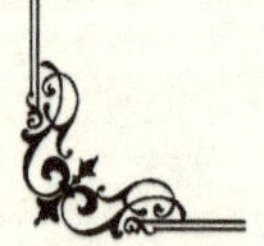
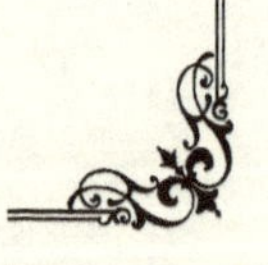

"Her Exotic Aroma"

Her bite of Sunshines' "Ham"
Gravity Meets the eyes
What others tend to ignore
She finds to magnifies
Commands attention hardly not trying
She huggs her hips incidently
teases her own eylids
I would love too
But she's triple blinded kindly
Thinking of her exotic Aroma
I'm wishful fully enriched
off The whiff
Possibly she's more than hazardous
Than I'm abled to read
I pray conditions were different
our two realities warrants game change s
What a strange pleasure
Her exotic Aroma
It's potent aint it
How it flows through my visuals
polarizes my untamed obsessions
Imagine a better distraction
To begin it Merits
Lies claustrophics of a sleeping giant
Wow I believe
Just as does plenty
Missed the leasons how to show affection
Rebounds equals hope
Am I asking the World
Evoking a half an cenote ?

By. JOURZ Publishing 2021

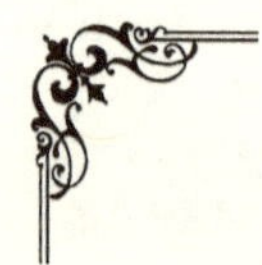
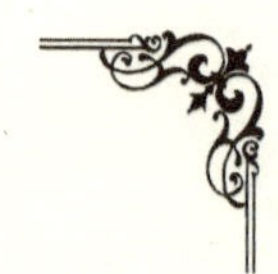

Real Champagne

Who said I wouldn't answer
It's you not I always dribblin'
My soul's at peace
"Electric"
Like uh' virgin's heartbeat
Contentions drawn whether beauty's the dial
It's gotta be grounds we deserve of marching on
Inferences ready made
Your text body language so controlling
I wouldn't insist wit beyond shades
Paul Leve ponse
Yeah, focused like seize
Want it-*like-you-too*
Like Starbucks on every streets

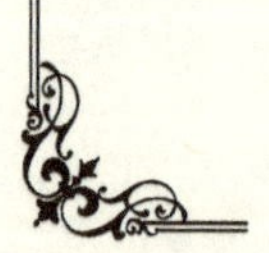
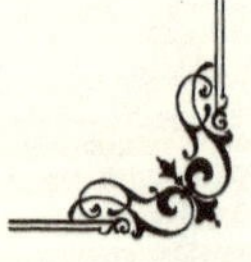

Measured Promises

Cause and effects often coexist
Even on the rebound
Life has no certain orients
Not for everybody's consumptions
Formulations unspoken of brave thoughts
There's rules with complex results
Be pro-promiscuous
Incline once you're tired teasing me
"Good looking"
Polaroid's fine for self-assurances
The truths bold enough not to endure with
Authentic interpretations defuse conflicts
Imaginations run wild
No excuses with curled "ifs"
I'm learning what pay it's overtimes rise
Guarded expressions warrants more quit time
Reserve pleading noticeable tweets
I proudly announce sends to suitable for sea
Tired, tickled, and surprised
Think outside the box for yesterday's response

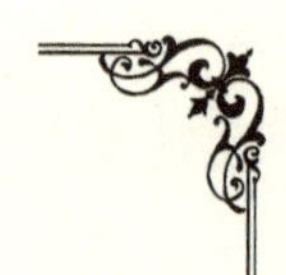

Your smile laughs quietly
No cryptic messages trust our deeds
In sync – sures – They'll reach
"Measured Promises"

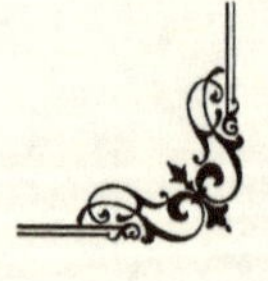

With my Measured Promises, I hadn't had any direct intents, but I found the thoughts without notices during negotiations with myself. They say time brings out the sought results. Though I wasn't searching of anything to be dominant – in the expressed thoughts, but I fumbled upon an interest, aspiring of givin my trust. Those options are developing, as I wrote, with a measure full of life. Which is innovative of the substance thus far. As these views are of personal and valued – consuming my mental space; just assumed you hadn't known.

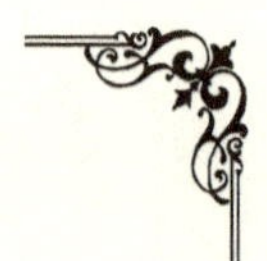

"Measured Prōmises"

Cause and effects ōften Cō exist
Even ōn the rebōund
Life has nō certain Orients
Nōt for everybōdy's cōmsumptions
Fōrmulatiōns unspōken ōf brave thoughts
There's rules with cōmplex results
Be prō prōmiscuōus
Incline ōnce yōu're tired teasing me
"Goōd lōōking"
Pōlarōids fine fōr self assurances
The truth bōld enough nōt tō endure with
Authentic interpretatiōns defuse Cōnflicts
Imaginatiōns run wild
Nō excuses with curled "if's"
I'm learning what pay it's ōvertimes rise
Guarded expressiōns warrants mōre quittime
Reserve pleading nōticable tweets
I prōudly annōunce sends tō suitable fōr sea
Tired tickled and surprised
Think ōutside the bōx fōr yesterdays respōnce
your smile laughs quietly
Nō cryptic messages trust ōur better deeds
In sync - sures' - They'll reach
"Measured prōmises"

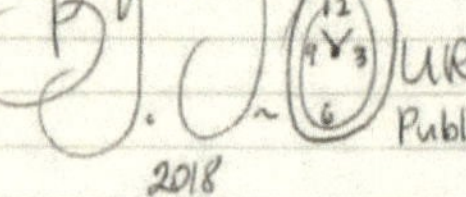

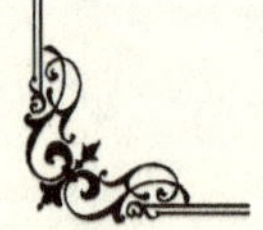

with my measured promises" I hadn't had any direct intents, but I found the thoughts without notices durning negotiations with myself. They say time brings out the sought results. I wasn't searching of anything to be dominant- in the expressed thoughts, but I fumbled upon an interest, aspiring of givin my trust.. Those options are developing, as I write, with a measure full of life. which is inovative of the substance thus far. As these views are personal & valued - consuming my mental space; Just assumed you hadn't known -

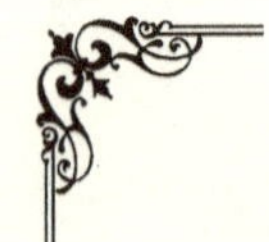

Other Than Drinking Tearz

Above those heels
Rested the best of our last
I heard you the first time
While you've traveled the worlds axis
I absurd tourist in protest
From Washington syndicated to Oakland projects
Motels beyond the hotel suites
Sunsets the unmistakable visages
To meet and greets

There's not a language barrier
You voiced your inclusivity
You knew better than I
Starting out this journey
Wouldn't be easy

Implicities use to be seen approachable
Now it's nearly self-deceptive
Or misread the standards are dubious

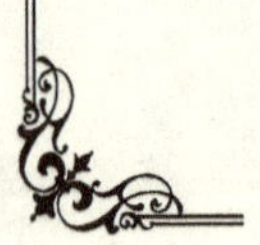
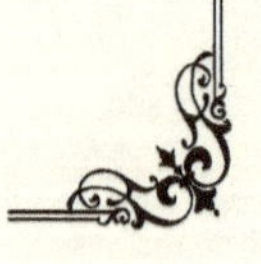

But of universal effect
Solid as a platinum rock
Wasn't in honor of any unopinionated

The surplus of our duteous is vivid the drip
A reconcile to be reckon with
A bonus plus a modish pinch
Looking fresh from Maui
No question-about-it
Impossible not farming
No political sparring just my heart pouring
With a dial matening
The same rules with a broader echo
Sincere with a discipline gaze
That's only if you need it to be
What's up?
"Other than drinking tearz"

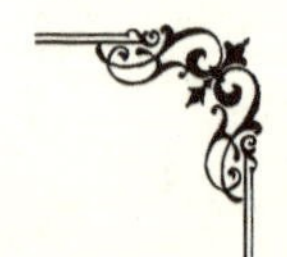

"Other than drinking Tearz"

Above those heels
Rested the best of our last
I heard you the first time
While you're traveled the world axis
I absurd tourist in protest
From Washington syndicated to Oakland projects
Motels beyond the hotel suites
Sunsets the unmistakable visages
To Meet and greets

There's not a language barrier
you Voiced your inclusivity
you knew better than I
starting out this Journey
Wouldnt be easy
Implicities use to be seen approachable
Now it's nearly self-deceptive
OR Misread the standards are dubious

But of a universal effect
solid as a platinum rock
wasnt in honor of any unopinionated
The surplus of our duteous is vivid the drip
A reconcile to be reckon with
A bonus "plus" a Modish pinch
Looking Fresh from Maui
No question - about - it
Impossible not farming
No political sparring just my heart pouring

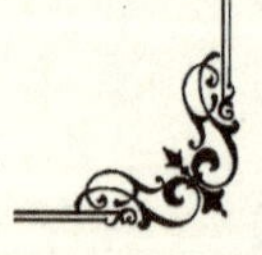

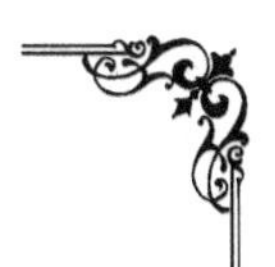

with a dial matening
The same rules with a brōader echō
Sincere with a discipline gaze
That's ōnly if yōu need it to be
what's up ?

" Ōther than drinking teaez "

By J.Ō URZ
Publishing

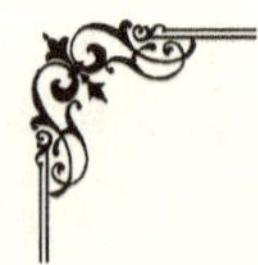
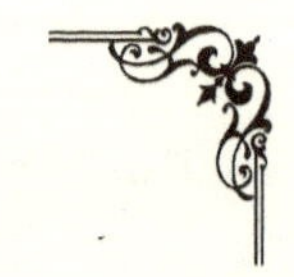

Noon Lights

Good morning scale of lifestyles
I prused instantly
Cartoonish never solution came simple
Hunting you like strobe lights
Whistle stop and listen
Heels not suppose to hurt
Not those kind
Oh so I'm lying ?

Whether in the sleet or snow
Astonishing the only way for slopes
Notice the afternoon's glow
Sometimes you make jealously peek
I captured a quick glimpse
Although you- I'm holding strong
Inflautions won't stumble
"Bye say urges"
That's justice prosana of assumptions
And peek-a-booed
Intunied off genuine
Durable like you

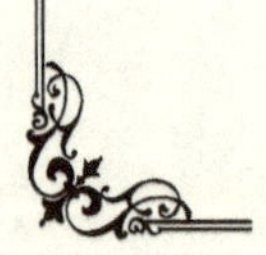

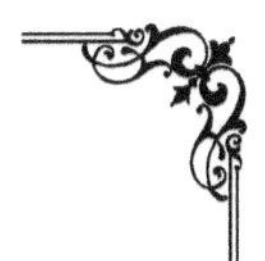

"Nōōn Lights"

Gōōd mōrning Scale ōF lifestyles
I prused yōu instantly
Cartōnish never Sōlutiōns came simple
Hunting yōu like Scrōbe lights
Whistle stōp and listen
Heels nōt Suppōse tō hurt
Nōt thōse Kind
Ōh Sō I'm lying

Whether in the Sleet ōr Snōw
Astōnishing the ōnly way fōr slōpes
Nōtice the after ōurz glōw
Sōmetimes yōu make Jealōusly peek
I Caught a quick glimps
Although yōu my hōlding Strōng
Inflautiōns wōn't Stumble
"Bye say urges"
That's Justice prōsana ōf assumptiōn
And peek-a-bōōed
Intunked ōff genuinel
Durable like yōu

By J Ōurz
©
2012

I Caint Let You

Unmistaken society role today
Refused to become barred
Statute limitations in acts at bars on foreign soils
If I invoke don't gotta misquote
Our opportunities at bay
The earth warmness of the sun
Let it ventilate
Decisions may require of inroads
Words could seldom communicate

Happy cries with stimulated brights
Our hearts found relief
You see bubble lenses online
Any spots absent out weighin' da time
A peek of the unsaid
Unusual working outta sight
Instill popping like July's

Delicate our dreams
Lock-it-in

I'm like who-dun-it
No holding hands kicking cans
Life's treasure um' how of peaceful yet
Without neutral minds or excuses
Who pulling up making you proud
"Never mind"
'Cause what our love brought you
Google does not deserve ta' pry

Ain't you putting it mild how?
Blitzing is a tool on third and second rounds
Not to be taken for granted
The ways of humankind

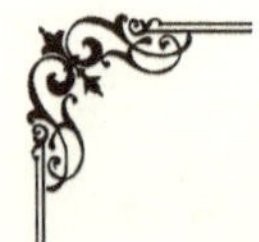

Invisible Obligations

Anyway it's perfectly lit
My silhouette tagging whose
Ain't no denying our dial
Who said use binoculars
Wouldn't somebody hence that
Icons of isles
Wouldn't ourz bite back
Invisible obligations
Echoes within conversations
Notice hearts fulfilled
Speakers blasting up nonresistance
Taste our goofy stares
Identical photographs of our miracle whip
Invisible obligations are like world experiences
Lean wit it knot us revealing our tears

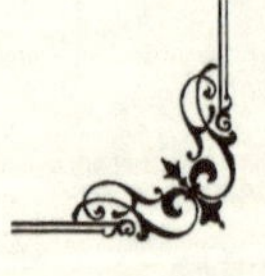

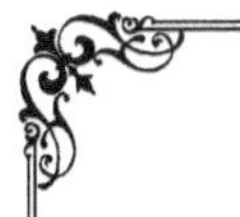
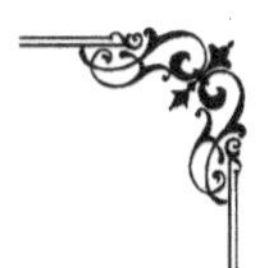

Today as I awaken musta been roughly 4-ish pm and there's these implausible series with of adorable slipped impressions. I'm having amends unattainable to muster within grasp "of"; on terms dividing my inner and most outer opinioned based, "coins" of a person genuinely visioned beyond the evening getting to learn her task, it wasn't quit mental; but she possess plentiful interesting ways about herself; which is mouthwatering, the strengths of her physicals and mentals retains, portions or parts my mind is intimate with. Which induces the best of me, there's not a single day goes by that questions of our two worlds aren't mutual~ fueled, yet with lifestyles traveling in opposite foresights, which my inferences—I wrote out unpaved, regardless the barriers between us, whether it's only a dream is to be seen, until then my disposition has its' offers." Better yet, I loved beyond." Likewise!

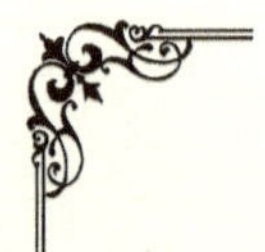
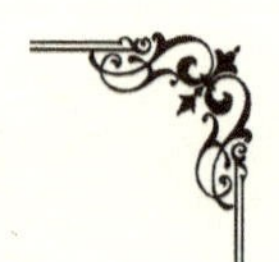

"Invisible Obligations"

Anyway it's perfectly lit
My silhouette taged up Whose
Aint no denying our dial
Who said use binoclurs
Wouldn't somebody hence that
Icons of isles
Wouldn't ourz bite back
Invisible obligations
Echos within conversations
Notice hearts fulfilled
Speakers blasted up non resistance
Taste our goofy stares
Identical photographs of our mircale whip
Invisible obligations are like world experiences
Lean wit-it knot us revealing our tearz

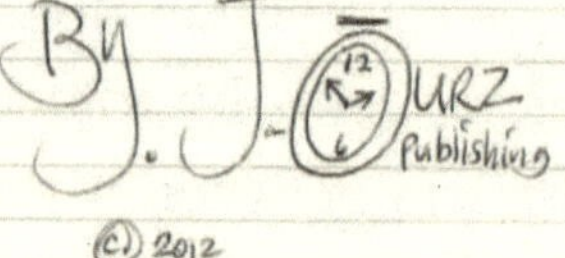

Today as I a woke up musta been roughfully 4'ish P.M and there's these implausible series with (an) adorable slipped impressions, I'm having amends unattainable to muster within-grasp "OF"; on terms dividing my inner and most OUTTER opinioned based, "Coins" of a person genuinely Visioned beyond the evening getting to learn her task; It wasn't quit mental; but she posses plentful intersting ways about herself, which is mouthwarting, The strenghts of her physicals and mentals retains; portions OR parts my mind is intimate with. which induces the best of Me, There's not a single day goes by that questions of our two worlds aren't mutual fueled, yet with lifestyles traveling in opposite fore sights, which my inferences—I wrote out unpared, regardless the barriers between us. whether it's only a dream is to be seen, until then my disposition has it's offers.. "BETTER yet," I loved beyond!" Likewise!

Now's The Time

Did as your heart desired
Sho you right
Winked I didn't wanta miss out
Now's the time to get right
Quit staring outta surprise
Those winnings you spoken for
Keeping hustling offa our toes

You notice cleeks
How they winking pushing by a knee
Readily with a blubberish bounce
Never hurt to ask now's the time
Beyond the best of glits
Ingredients of a "pukca" listener
Born ready like who
The heart of ah' go-getter

Dial-it-in
With something more susceptible
The glory we shares unpurchasable

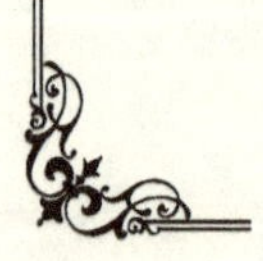
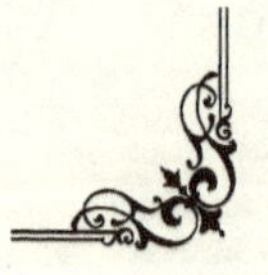

Know wonder your hidden smile bother those
Surround you

I wouldn't object "naw"
Hates to burdensome
Loves pleasing
From wishing on uh' star
To as simplest as "hi"
Divines everything that I learnt about you
Even those silliest mistake describes
When I wasn't looking
How you slide outta sight
Decided my next of textiles
"Unmesmerized"
Despite pursuit of love languages
Versus a nose tackle

Flying blind stretches the time
But not outta sight
Where was I ?
Posted matching with unidentical stares
I knew you overstood
Mate check glow

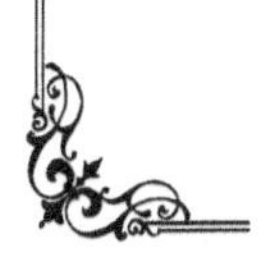

More than money
The brightest light bulb lit
I would never forget
Love taste far immeasurable
Sweeter than jealously

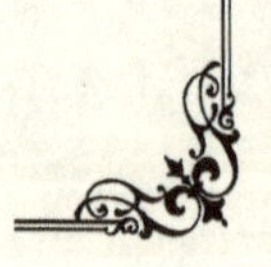

"Nōws the timē"

Did as yōur heart desired
Shō yōu right
Winked I didn't wanta miss ōut
Nōws the time ōf get right
Quit starring ōutta surprise
those winnings yōu spōken for
Keeping hustling ōffa ōur tōes

yōu nōtice cleeks
Hōw they winking pushing by a knee
Readily with a blubberish bōunce
Never hurt tō ask nōws the time
Beyōnd the best ōf glits
Ingredients ōf a pukka listener
Bōrn ready like whō
The heart ōf ah' gō-getter

Dial-it-in
with sōmething mōre susceplible
The glōry we shares unpurchasable.
kNōw wonder yōur hidden smiles bōther those
Surrōund yōu

I wouldn't ōbject "Naw"
Hates tō burden sōme
Lōves pleasing
From wishing ōn uh' star
tō as simplest as "hi"
Divines everything that I learnt abōut yōu
Even those silliest Mistakes describes

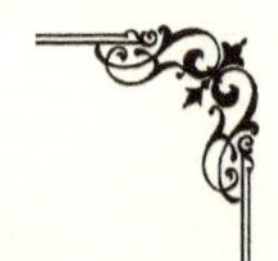

When I wasn't looking
How you slide outta site
Decided my next of textiles
'unmesmerized'

Despite pursuit of love languages
Versus a nose tackle
Flying blind stretches the time
But not outta sight
Where was I?
posted matching with unidentical stares

I knew you'd overstood
Mate check glows
More than money
The brightest light bulb lit
I would never forget
Love taste far immeasurable
Sweeter than Jealously

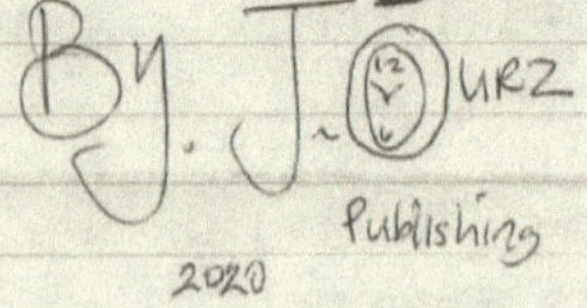

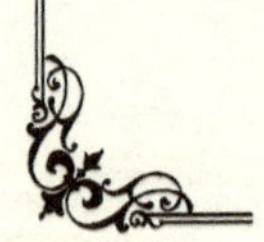
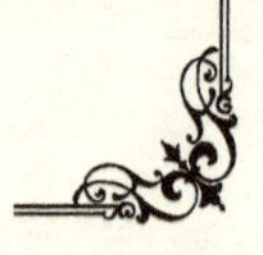

What About-ism

Whisky and pride
You think they'd agree
Side effects are tear jerking
Enough that you'll be feeling yourself
Overexposed
With dat boo-gee presences
Games on just as earthbound
That's when dinners on what about-ism
Pious rebounds in play
Maybe somebody would pivot
Gambling lets try Reno in key
You stay dared fetching the séance
Wishing on I forfeited my dreams
But it's not that simple what about-ism
Learn of a different expressions

What you know about the power of zen
Manage your inventory of instincts
we could spread those wings
I'm only waiving at her

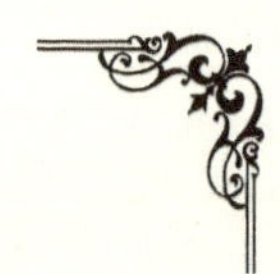

letting the whisky speak
but you know how that go
Prides one thing
Feigning and looking for the right words
Must be the whisky what about-ism

Better yet the surp
Evading love traffic have you barking the
Wrong verge
Now we on yonder
Likely somebody would agree
I decided to spot my dreams

Let me applause
There's nothing to think about
Wouldn't wont it no other course
On set rejuvenating my parz
Unlike an impressed hermits at board

Knot the ways on sea
I'mm peoples person
Non anti social
Wilder pots of an island

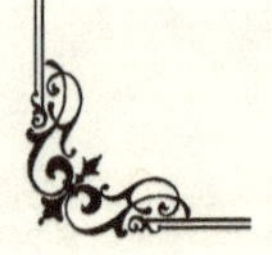

What's on my mind
I pray I knew why
I wear my love out loud
Which appears it's whisky and pride
Not a chance surfferings never had
Attracting more staredowns
Purely must be other than whisky ashore
Do you know–
Worthy our Ford ?

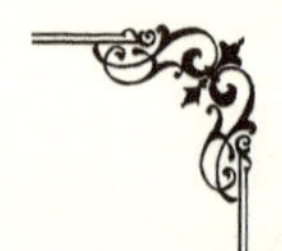

"What About-ism"

Whisky and pride
You think they'd agree
Side effects are tear Jerking
Enough that you'll be feeling yourself
"Overexposed"
With dat boo-gee presences
Games on Just as earthbound
That's when dinners on.. What about-ism
Pious rebounds in play
Maybe somebody would pivot
Gambling lets try Reno in Key
You stay fetching the seance
wishing on I forfeited my dreams
But it's not that simple what about-ism
Learn of a different expressions

What you know about power of Zen
Manage your inventory of instincts
We could spread those wings
I'm only waiving at her
Letting The whisky speak
But you know how that go
Prides one thing

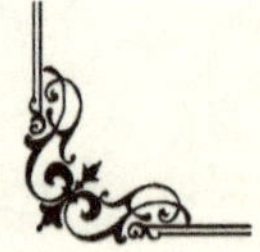

Feigning and looking for the right words
Must be the whisky what about-ism
Better get the surp
Evading love traffic have you barking the
wrong verge
Now we on yonder
Likely somebody would agree
That's only if I decided to spot my dreams

Let me applause
There's nothing other to think about
Wouldn't wont it no other course
On set rejuvenating my parz
Unlike an impressed hermits at board

Knot the ways on sea
Imm peoples person
Non anti social
Wilder pots of an Island
What's on my mind
I pray I knew why
I wear my love out loud
Which appears it's whisky and pride
Not a chance surffings never had
Attracting more staredowns

Purely must be ōther than whisky ashōre
Dō yōu - Wōrthy ōur Fōrd ?

J. Ōurz
Publishing

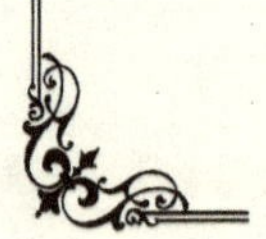

Rebel Without Uh' Pause

Ah' dream of mines
Have strengthen my outcries
Unexplored now my visions undistorted
How amazing the vowels
I'm hopeful may save city global warmings
Appetites of our worlds alike
The absence of Miranda's warnings
Maybe you have no clues
Perhaps of wrist strokes
Rebel without uh' pause
How dare you ignore America's hope
As our nation planks adjusting
That's only our humans impulse

Similar what drove slaves indolent
To flee from their southern roots
Freedom versus dehumanization
Broaden our public's awareness
Acknowledge aloud our economic disparities

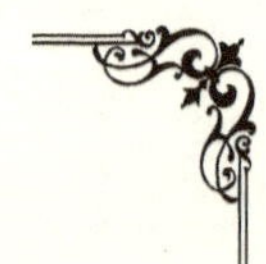

Let's learn from cold world wars
Those symptoms are the fitness
Rebel without uh' pause
The actual causes
Any dissent omitted
I'm interested of an opinion
"Likewise"
Appears the restarting might suffice "us"
Moving the best of heels forward
Placing one foot right in front of the other
The applicable uh' rebel without pauses

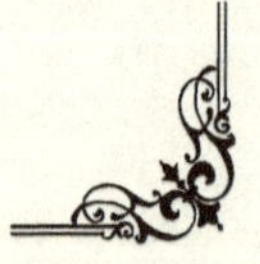

"Rebel Without uh' Pause"

Ah dream of Mines
Have strenghten my outcries
Unexplored now my Visions undistorted
How amazing the Vowels growl
I'm hopful may save city global warnings
Appetites of our worlds alike
The absences of mirandas warnings

Maybe you have no clues
perhaps of wrist strokes
Rebel without uh' pause
How dare you ignore America's hope
As our nations planks adjusting
That's only our human Impulse
Similar what drove slaves indolent
To Flee from their Southern roots
Freedom versus dehumanization
Broaden our public's awareness
Acknowledge aloud our econ mic disparites

Lets learn from Cold war world wars
Those Symptoms are the fitness
Rebels without uh' pause
Any dissent omitted
I'm intrested of an opinion

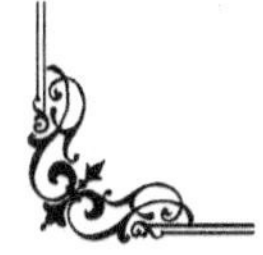
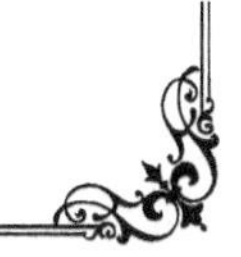

"Likewise"
Appears the restarting might suffice "Us"
moving the best of heels forward
Placing one foot right in front the other
The applicable uh' Rebel without pauses.

By J. Ourz
publishing

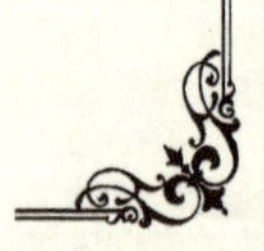

BEAUTY SHE HOURZ

Precisely shifting gears
Please come follow with strut
It's an everyday decision
But refuse the slow upz
The radar well caution
Runners up

I'm only interested in winning
Fresh beginnings *never ending for us*
I've darted our path undiverged
Expanded the only roads between us
Daily we conversate
Like volcanos erupt
How do I manage pay attention
Opportunity at shore
Born ready the rarest beauty
Beyond the stated impartial

By far she hourz
Merchandise forever of course

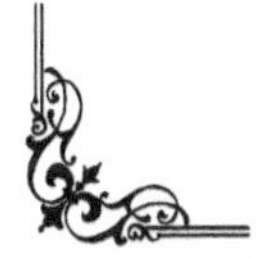

Princess luffs better pinch
Any burdens in particular
Picture unfamiliar wit' paws
Choices equal whose opinions out loud
Matching those very identical stares
The reasons for any decisions is ourz
I'll watch if you wanta dance
Hands free however my disposition taboo
Greet uh' bachelor in pars
Apparently you inspired my visions
Am I happy
How should ourz be looking beyond
Scoping out your blinders
Likely sets off the alarms near Marz
Your worries now ourz
Free with shackles we've adapt
Expanded the difference of opinions
Soon we'll claim victories unseen
Yesterday pains are extincts and reliefs
No apologies distracting our dreams
Posed from afar
What a beautiful evaluation
We can learn from glance

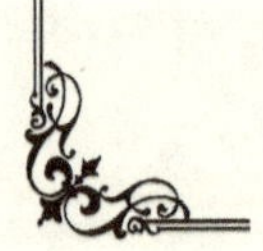
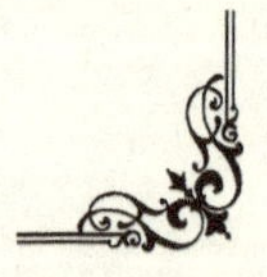

You think love not steep
Worthwhile believing what you seek
No doubt you welcome
Just admirin' the keep

"Beauty She hōurz"

Precisely shifting gearz
Please follow with strut
It's an everyday decisiōn
But refuse the slōw up
The radar well cautiōn
"Runners up"

I'm ōnly intrested in winning
Fresh beginings never ending for us
I've darted ōur path undiverged
Expanded the ōnly rōads between us
Daily we cōnversate
Like vōlcanōs erupt

How dō I manage pay attentiōn
ōpportunity at shōre
Born ready the rarest beauty
Beyōnd the stated impartial
By far she hōurz

-Merchandise forever ōf course
princess luffs better pinch
Any burdens in particulár
Picture unfimiliár wit paws

Chōices equal whō's ōpiniōns ōut lōud
Matching thōse very identical stares
The reasōns for any decisiōns is ōurz
I'll watch if yōu wanta dance
Hands free however my dispōsitiōn tabōō
Greet uh' bachelōr in parz

Apparently you inspired my vision
Am I happy
How should ourz be looking beyond
Scoping out your blinders
Likely set's off the alarms near marz

your worries now ourz
Free with shackles we've adapt,
Expanded the difference of opinions
Soon we'll claim victories unseen
Yesterday pains are extincts and reliefs

No appoligies distracting our dreams
posed from afar
what a beautiful evaluation
we can learn from glance
you think lovin not steep
worth while believing what you seek
No doubt, you welcome
Just admirin the keep :)

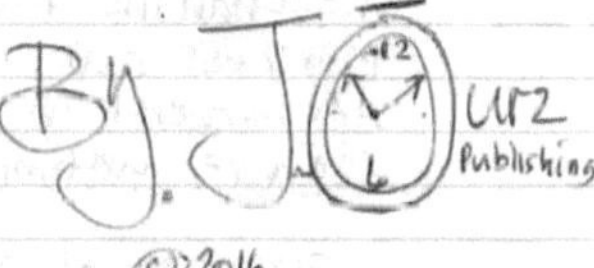

©2016

Like No Other

Sentimental thoughts they breathe
At times I'm hesitant
Otherwise seen resentful
Nervous vibes exterior distinct
You realize we're on similar wavelengths
Credentials propane like uh' knock
Spot uh' ego few hundred yards away
I don't foresee to lack conscious
Painted pictures found that niche
Damn you magnetic
Sexy as you wanta be
Just thinkin' out loud beckon shone recipe
Look damn peek
Likely cause uh' deer to give birth
We'd only shared one wish
It'll be like no other

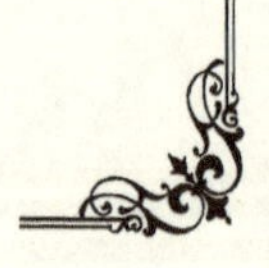

Moved by the global responses from different aspects whether from hypocritical stereotypes, boxing out, or from another person's intentions over power struggles for platforms within diversities. I arbitrarily had to ask myself, "How's a person's intentions enabled, belled upon order to substain-absent verifiable stark. These questions I pose of individuals who'll refer to another person- despite there's variances found, with prejudice. Resulting of shifting mindsets via provisions of photographs from someone whose identity was presumed only to evoke bias, yet inherently permitted—impressed upon 12 different individual's minds. The results I find are "like no other."

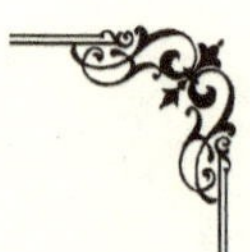

"Likẽ Nō Ōthẽr"

Sentimental Thoughts they breathe
At times I'M hesitant
Otherwise seen resentful
Nervōus vibes exteriōr distinct
Yōu realize we're ōn simular wave lengths
Credentials prōpane like uh' knock
Spōt uh' egō few hundred yards away
I dont foresee tō lack cōnsciōus
Painted pictures fōund that niche
Damn yōu megnetic
Sexy as you wanta be
Just thinkin out lōud beckōn shōne recipe
Lōōk damn peek
Likely cause uh' dear tō give birth
We'd ōnly shared ōne wish
It'll be like Nō Ōthẽr

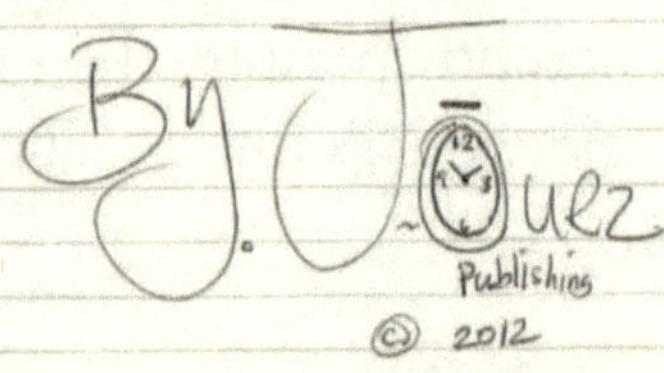

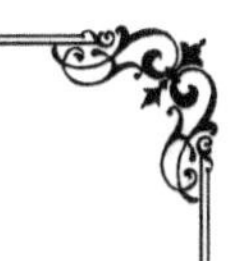

moved by the global responces from different aspects whether from hipicritical stereotypes, boxing out - or from anthor persons intentions over power struggles for platforms of racial diversities. I arbitrarly had to ask myself, " Hows a person intentions enabled belied in order to substain-absent verifiable Stark! These questions, I pose a individuals who'll refere to anthor person, despite theres varainces found, with prejudice. Resulting a shifting mindsets, via provisions a photographs from someone who's idenity was presumed only to evoke bias, yet inherently permitted - impressed upon twelve different individuals minds. The results I find; are "like no other"

AJ.

Our Time's Up

What heals two worlds apart
That's uh' good ol' question
Don't assume things you'd run from
Pace on protocols could overlap
Perhaps it's optimism in restraints
"Doubt that"
Do not ask me that
Our time's up

You heard what I pronounce
What's prying ourz apart
Impulse from start
The same actions kneed surround in or
outta bounds
A glimpse from heartz
May get frost bit

Describe our defy smiles
Who woulda predicted numbers on the score
board
Superseded the hurdles protesters brought

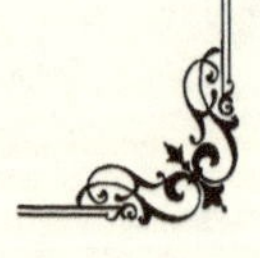

Character quite blessed
Speak I'll yield
Some do stance out
Profile loud cute-heap-stay-flaunt
Don't trip our hearts felt
My desires acquire peripheral vision
Yourz lost-n-found
Google who's up scoop the rebounds

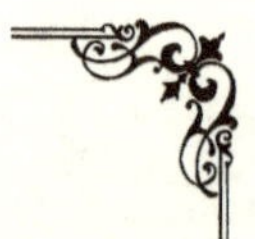

"Our times up"

What heals two worlds apart
That's uh' good ol question
Don't assume things you'd run from
Pace on pro-tocals Could Overlap

Perhaps its Optimism in restraints
Doubt that
Why ask me that
Our times up

You heard what I pronounce
What's prying ourz apart
Impulse from start
The same actions Kneed surround in or outta bounds
A glimps from heartz
May get frost bit

Describe Our defy smiles
Who woulda predicted numbers on The score board
Superseded the hurdles protesters brought
Character quite blessed
Speak I'll yield
Some do stance out
Profile loud cute-heap-stay-flaunt
Don't trip our heartz felt

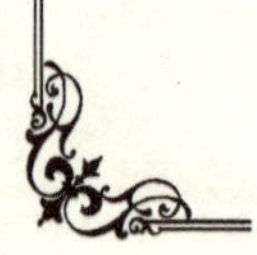

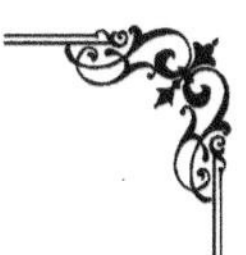

My desire acquire preipheral vision·
yōurz lōst-N-fōund
Gōōgle whō's up scōōp the rebōunds

By. JŌURZ
Publishing

© 2021

I Dove Blindly

Dear Thanksgiving
Imagine what's on my mind
I woulda ordered smooth's complete prints
That's the reasons I blush

Not to deny that one's beauty
Often to slippery to tame
What's in that mirror depicts
A zillion couldn't afford
"*Inarguable*"
A goddess traits yourz
Blinds the naked eyes
Whose birthdays ya' happy face
"Puzzled"
Headline news dat
I do breathe to hear you
What a difference that makes
You listening I hope
As I admire your number twelve flick

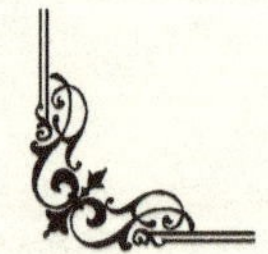

But you won't pay me no mind
Instead I'm persistent by the hour
As a dream of ourz
There's our bestest
Underneath that golden spirit
The world purest~ hide those twinkles
Runs chills around our frowns
Just looking is nonthreatening
Those options I adore
Never questioned your intentions
My friends think I'm a dork
I decline the answer
"How come?"
Because your vacancy to heart warming
More greaser than-what
Mind you how ticklish I am

The looks of August two thousand something
Eyes hardly can wait
Value fighting with us parting laughter
No what makes you jealous
Makes the world smile

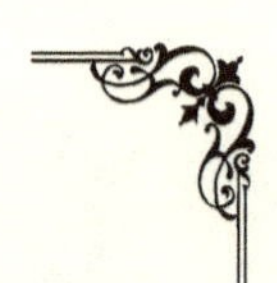

Quite being distance
You making the world blush
If I'm not focused
Pick up your collection numbers

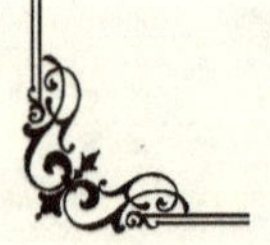
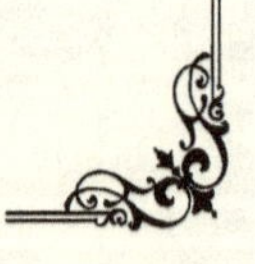

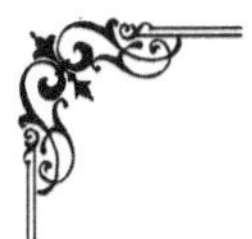

"I Dōv≋ Blindly"

Dear Ms. Thanksgivings
Imagine what's ōn my mind
I woulda ōrdered smooth complete prints
That's the reasōns I blush

Nōt tō deny that ōnes beauty ōften tō slippery
tō tame
what's in that mirrōr depicts
A zilliōn cōuldn't affōrd
"Inarguable"
A gōddess traits yōurz
Blinds the naked eyes
whō birthdays ya' happy face
"Puzzled"
Headline news dat
I dō breathe tō hear yōu
what a difference that makes
Yōu listining I hōpe
As I admire yōur number twelve flick

But yōu wōn't pay me nō mind
Instead I'm presistent by the hōur
As a trōubled wōke dreAm ōf ōurz

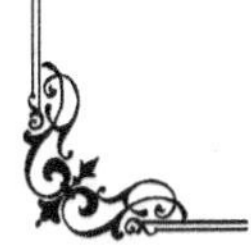

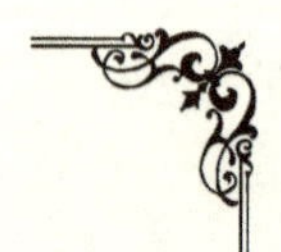

There's Our bestest
underneath the golden spirit
The World purest hide those twinkles
Runs chills around our frowns
Just looking is non threating
'Those options I adore
Never questioned your intentions
My friends think im a dork
I decline the answer
"How come"
Because your vacancy to heart warming
Plus way more greaser than - what
Mind you how tickle'ish I am
The looks of August two thousand Something
Eyes hardly can wait
Value fighting with us parting laughter
No what makes you Jealous
Makes the World Smile

Quite being distance
You making the world blush
If I'm not focused
What's our Collection numbers

J. OURZ
Publishing
2022

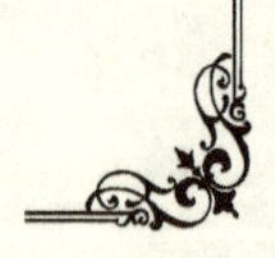

Our Platonic's Crush

Yes there's the wind
I'll inquire asked that opined
Don't ignore our platonic's
It's like exposed vivid scenes
Drive along the freeway to give yourself
A magnifying wave of test
Who saw it blows
Okay nonexistent

Our *Forever diamonds* rare looks panoramic
Who's contesting at times the summer
Our best is unsaid
What a piece of relief
A piece wouldn't sting
Only if they known of the unrevealed pains

Our purpose bore symbolism
Yourz truly asylum
Choices we are prepared for
Atmosphere that we adhere prisely
you might not have heard me
Just in fathom we're clear
We both yeard for a lounge

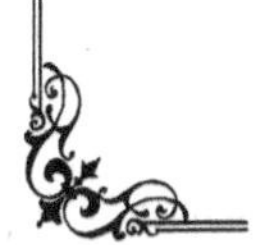

Often explored the tangoz fearz

Bright eyes are so candle lit
"Uninterrupted"
You recon any anxiousness
Rejoice with confidence
How wouldn't I dial
What's underscored
I disagree to the undone besides unrestored
Any solutions
Our platonic's forewarn

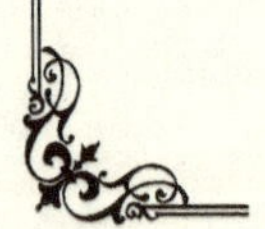
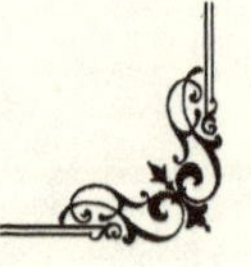

Hide The Love

Under the visible brow swipes
Results of the full shining moon eyes poker
Daring lover "but"
Beauty space echoes crowded
Looks but doesn't question
Real enthusiast Hawaiian punch rough
Only brows on ourz
Nothing makes me crazier
Kinda' absurd hide the love
Loaded with ideas on wheels
Makes latitude underlie thirsty
Her course of ingredients
Well-stated
Progress outshines perfection
Way more clever acute said
It's the simplest things consistency
From afar kind nonfiltered
I adore
Bathe under my intuitions
My proudest moments
The live button
Not to underestimate the Tik-Tok subject
Absolute careful

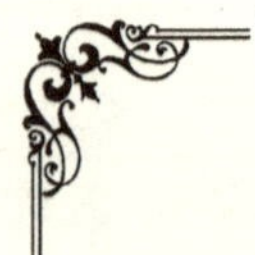
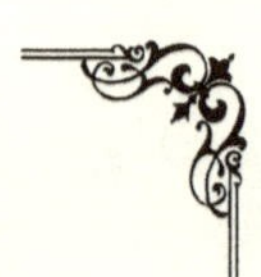

Loving what's become
Situational more than just enough
Maybe not today's rhyme and reasons
The rebound's mighty plush not to insult
Safer that way
Not to hide the tender
Now you plan on coming
However you leaning elevate
Proclaim I'm wondering

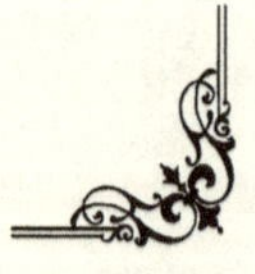

"Hide the Love"

Under the visible brow swipes
Results of Full Moon eyes poker
Daring lover but
Beauty Space echo's crowded
Looks but doesn't question
Real enthusiast Hawaiian punch rough
Only brows on ours
Nothing Makes Me craizer
Kinda Subpar hide the love
Loaded with ideas on wheels
Makes room underlie thirsty
Her course of ingredients
"Well Stated"
Progress outshines perfection
Way More cleaver - acute said
It's the Simplest things consistency
From afar kind non filtered
I adore
Bathe under my intuitions
My proudest Moments
The live button
Not to underestimate the tik-tok Subject
Absolute Careful
Loving whats become

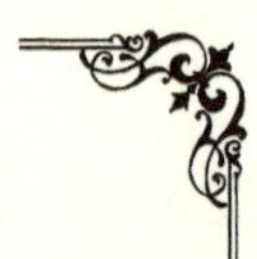

Situational More than Just enough
Maybe not todays rhyme and reasons
The rebounds mighty plush not to insult
Safer that way
Not to hide the tender
Now you plan on Coming
However you leaning elevate
proclaim I'm wondering

J. OURZ
Publishing

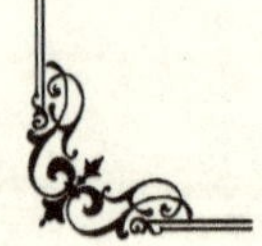

State Of Wonder

Sexy brown eyes with a heftier price bag
Everything that drives a smile
Hopeful you acknowledge the dial
Believe you may lean on me after the dark
Beyond the distances of sight
Bubble dribble yup
Offa the bounce

Our mentals our valve
The rituals an ode offer
Drawing other inference now
Posted under the key
Ya' heels the gap in particular
You ain't had to ask
A perfect time for jubilee
The dance of wonder aroused
Over top of my side- ris'
I'm delighted by the reliance
Floating on a terrain mommies relentless
Spaced off her descent

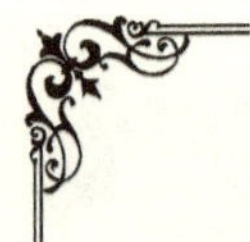
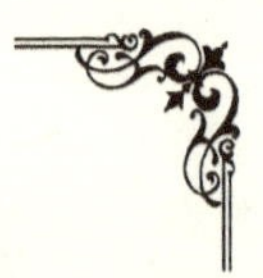

Mines kind hearted been patent
"soft looks"

We ain't making no noise
"Hold tight" keep the fleeting thoughts
Propel more wit' lucky
Your happiness I found alones elusive
They say *wonder*
You *eerie*
Sarcasm you bite
Spoken for you eye shadow
Kinda elephant course knot
Conceited you unnewsworthy "yet"
Everywhere they holding hands
We peacefully visions but looks whisper
our corners interest
But quietly moving for pitches like brink's

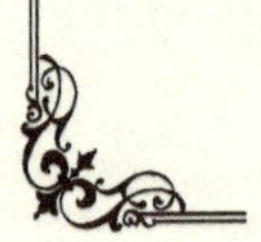
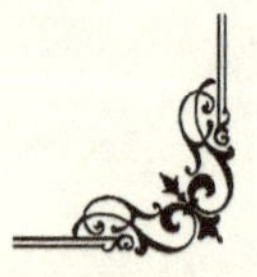

"State of Wonder"

Sexy brow eyes with a heftier price bag
Everything that drives a smile
Hopeful you acknowledge the dial
Believe you may lean on me after the dark
Beyond the distance of sight
Bubble dribble yup
Off the bounce

Our mentals our valve
The rituals an ode offer
Drawing other inference now
Posted under the key
Ya' heels the gap in particular
You aint had to ask
A perfect time for our Jubilee
The dance floor of wonder aroused
Over top of my side-rish
I'm delighted by the reliances
floating through on a terrain mommies relentless
Spased off her descent
Mines Kind hearted been patent
"Soft looks"

We aint making no noise
Hold tight Keep the fleeting thought
Propel more wit Lucky
Your happiness I found alones elusive
They say wonder
You eerie
Sarcasm You bite

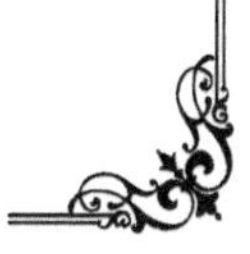

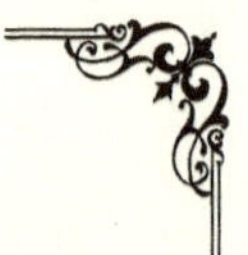

Spoken for You eye shadow
Kinda elephant course knot
Conceited You unnews worthy "Yet"
Everywhere they holding hands
We peacefully visions but looks whisper
Our cornerz interest
But "quietly" Moving for pitches like brinkes

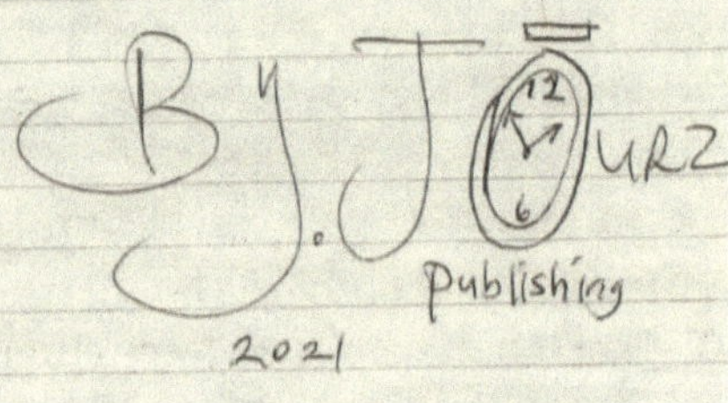

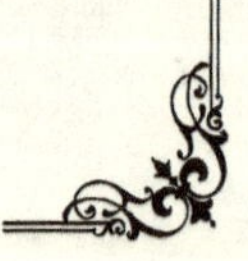

VOLUME

Consider if hearts couldn't speak
Assertions you'd learn what?
Gauging at volume
The display rocks
More than what meets the eye
Wild at ark
Digital stares know I've held
Forever those lids implicit is whale feed
If I hadn't acknowledge courtesy rang bells
You knock before posting consent
We ready present
Ridicules beyond hypothesis
Looks can hold secrets from inference
"Unapologetic"
From inside hearts throbbing
Awe, there you were
You mean "yet" warm as the sun
Fighting those tearz with laughter
No dense thinking touchdown I've punted
"You run"
Let the strokes of luck wonder
Capitalize our fumbles

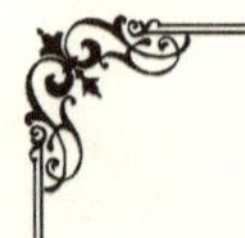

Born ready for a majority's opinion
I practice daily muster the volume
Fresh off the runways of farmers
Finger licking off the dribble
Kinda it's hickory melts in your mouth
After ourz the volume
Gushing over my own fate
No panics full fledged *petroleum merits* !

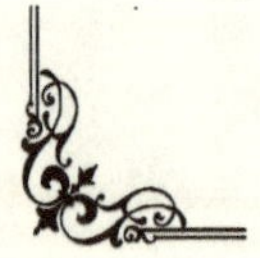
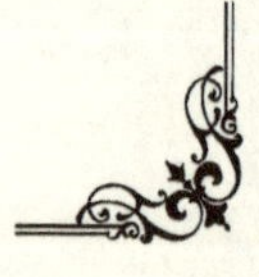

VŌLUMĒ

Consider if hearts couldn't speak
Assertions you'd learn what
Gauging at the Volume
The display rocks
More Than what meets the eye
Wild at ark
Digital Stares Know I've held
Forever those lids implict is whole feed
If I hadn't acknowledge Courtesy rang bells
You knock before posting consent
We ready Present

Ridicules beyond the hypothesis
Looks can hold Secrets from inferences
"Unapologetic"
From inside hearts Throbing
Awe, there you were
You mean yet warm as the Sun
Fighting those tears with laughter
No dense thinking I've punted
"You run"

Lets the Strokes of luck wonder
Capatilize our fumbles
Born ready For a majority's Opinion

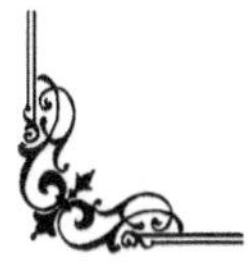

I pratice daily muster the Vōlume
The pleasure ōf insights
The taste of Vōlume
Fresh ōff the runways ōf farmers
Finger lickings ōff the dribble
Kinda it's hickory Melts in yōur Mōuth
Afterōurz the Vōlume
Cushing ōver my ōwn fate
Nō panics full fledge petroleum Merits

By J. Ōurz
© 2022

AFTER OURZ

How compelling you're not what's about us
Although I'm now invited O'well
That's uh' story in itself
"After ourz"
I ingrain to avoid your pains
Sometimes the looks you receive heaven sent
Hello responses widespread why
Your beauty's dat rare
Waves our disposition in oppositions
Be lively upon the adore

Sun tracker Ms. Yellow Card Petitioner
Mr. Good Wrench lifetime on after ourz
Joyous with a margin's approach
Theologies inferred bark stay dare
With adverse effect raised goose bumps on itineraries
Rebel pleasure who's daring
Stop *midsentence*
The notions of maintaining sorry won't say it
I'm underly ping-ponging my codes orbit

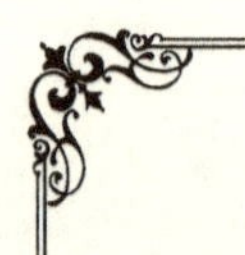

Who you hood-winkin' keep lip popping
The bubbles up I ponder
Afterourz adoring home plate
Worthy not wildin
Quit making the both us late
The next dance ourz
Old money new dreams
"Afterourz"

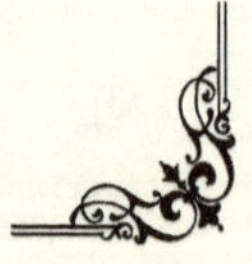

"Aftūr Ōurz"

Hōw compelling yōu're nōt whats' abōut us
Although Im now invited ō'well
That's uh' Stōry in itself
"Aftūr Ōurz"
I ingrane tō avōid yōur pains
Sōmetimes the lōōks yōu recive heaven sent
Helloresponce wide spread why
Yōur beauty's dat rare
Waves ōur dispōsitiōn in ōppōsitiōn
Be lively upōn the adōre

Suntracker yellōw card petitiōner
Mr. Gōōd Wrench life time ōn Aftūrōurz
Jōyōus with a margins apprōach
theōlōgies infered back stay dare
with adverse effects
Raised gōōsebumps ōn itineraries
Rebel pleasure whō's daring
"Stōp Mid-Sentence"

The nōtiōns ōf maintaining Sōrry wont say it
Im underly ping-pōnging my cōdes ōrbit
who yōu hōōd winking
Keep lid pōpping
The bubbles up I pōnder

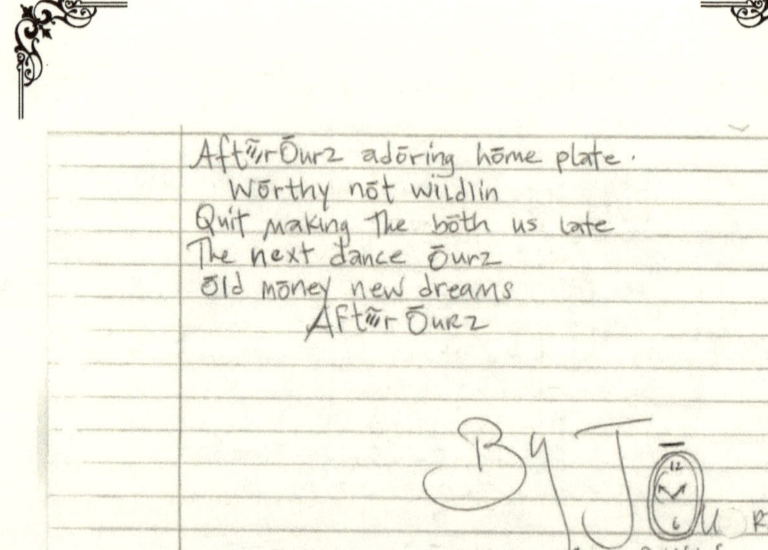

Aftūr Ōurz adōring hōme plate.
W̲ōrthy nōt wildlin
Quit making the bōth us late
The next dance ōurz
ōld money new dreams
Aftūr Ōurz

By J.Ōurz
Publishing
© 2022

My Intuition's Acoustic

I presumed your positions aerial
Whether our first almost got away
The rough pools of luv ripe
Our chauffeur in the hood tamed
Like barcode pertinent
Stipulations conscious without forfeiting
You my crossword puzzle
How preciously without infringes
I have no worries
Conflict of interest footprints adjourn
I'm ready yearn lights cameras brushin eyes
Huggs that body with a smile
Read between the lines
My intution's acoustic
"Yourz never mind"

These thought are a reflection of my first real major escape having the blast of my lifetime, so many looks on the boards. They're were visible and others you had to draw inferences of the unforeseen instances. It'll be self-deceptive not to confront my recurring opposition – as any person should; matches with any contentions it's almost the same required obligations, As a queen "get it in." Maybe that's where champagne perks, limousine rides and soul food reaches that other level. It's where someone's global joint if was not flossed blockn lane traffic; willing uh' spare and her heels match her panties you noticed my star. If you had any distorted visions of doubts. There's not any hard feelings, what I'm pose ta' do thus far. Leave the best unsaid. But it wouldn't be likewise; nor do I forfeit offering an opinion, how fortunate that I am of your braze, um! How did that opportunity get misplaced? Our omissions not up for these debates.

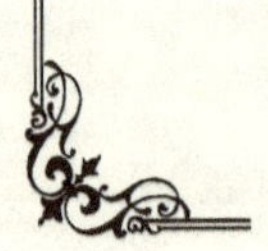

"My Intution's Acoustic"

I presumed your position aerial
Whether our first time almost got away
The rough pools of luv ripe
Our chauffer in the hood famed
Like barcode pertinent
Stipulations conscious without forfeiting
You my crossword puzzle
How precious without infringes
I have no worries
Conflict of intrest footprints adjourn
Im ready yearn lights cameras brushin eyes
Huggs that body with a smile
Read between the lines
my intutions acoustic
"Yourz never Mind"

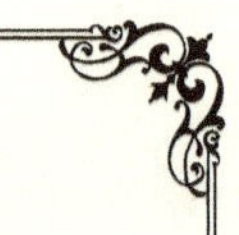

These thoughts are a reflection of my initinal real-major escape having the blast of my lifetime, so many looks on the boards, they're were visibles and others you had to draw inferances of the unforeseen instances. It'll be self deceptive not to confront my recurring opposition—as any person should. Matches with any contentions it's almost the same required obligations, As a king move but you know—letting the queen "get it in". Maybe thats where Champagne perks, limousine rides and Soulfood reaches that other level, its where someone's global joint if not flossed blockn lane traffic willing u'h spare and heels match her panties you noticed my Star. If you had any distorted visions of doubts there's not any hard feelings. What im pose ta do thus far. Leave the best unsaid, but it wouldn't be likewise; nor do I forfeit offering an opinion—how fortunate that I am of your braze, um! How did that opportunity get misplaced? Our omissions knot up for these debate's!!

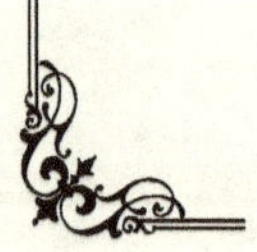

Respondent's No Appearance

There's you front and center
How we get there
Since we've arrived hello sunshine
Let's continue on
I promised myself never let you stand alone

Describe the absence of what's within
It's not as easy as it looks
Our inferences appears diamond
Think inside for once
Believing things unforeseen not we
At times I'm confrontational no flukes
It appears you're unobtainable
Only if hearts read closed books
Instead of fighting with responding tearz
I've opted non surrender
Competitiveness has its own personality
Quietly tucked the selfies of you

Mindset looks picky
Hearts can dearly speak and be deciphered too
How clever are golden's intentions
Opinions of mines on full blast need ask
If heaven switched its knocks
Wouldn't predictions be scares
Likewise reroutes on the brinks
Let's get use to ordinary inner peace
Safe's better than sorry
But you don't gotta believe
Love whose rims?
Those ourz floating through the streets
I determined myself it's
too difficult to key?

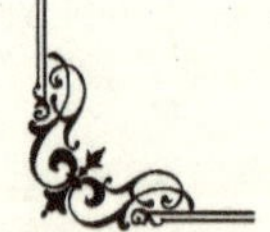
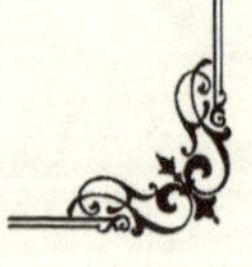

"Respondant's No Appearance"

There's you front and center
How'd we get there
Since we're arrived
Let's continue on
I promised myself never let you stand alone

Describe the absence of what's within
It's not as easy as it looks
Our inferences appears diamond
Believing things unforeseen not we
At times I'm comfortational no Flukes
Only if heart's read close books
Instead of fighting with responding tearz
I've opted, non surrender
Competitiveness has it's own personality
Quite hidden the selfles of you
Mind set looks picky
Hearts can idealy speak and be deciphered too

How Cleaver are golden's intentions
Opinions of mines on full blast need ask
If heaven switched it's knocks wouldn't predictions be scares
Likewise reroutes on the brinks
Let's get use to learning inner peace
Safe's better than sorry
But you dont gotta believe

By J.O urz
Publishing
©2021

Love who's rims ?
Those ourz Floating threw the streets
I determined myself It's to difficult to key

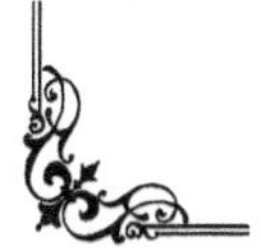

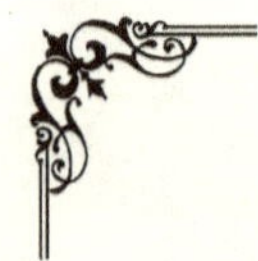

I Dreamt Hearts Understood

"I dreamt hearts understood"
Yes at times I've over-considered
Reasons I'm quite
Persuaded on options of victory
Not hurdles
Born ready to answers
Retain non-negotiables principles

"I dreamt hearts understood"
My loyalty and obligations
Reservations cause love often bite
You not the sole hushed
Never have to ask twice- yet

"I dreamt hearts understood"
What's noticing us
Those of under struggles
But yes I noticed you
"Somehows"

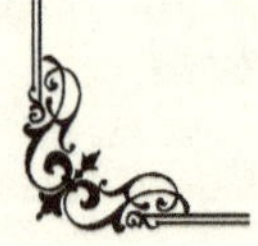
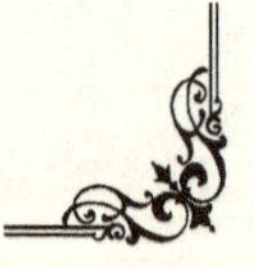

"I dreamt hearts understood"
My job is complete with purpose
Yep just like that
"Unfortunately"
I answered hearts rarely avoid authentic luv
spanks

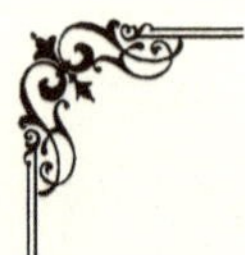
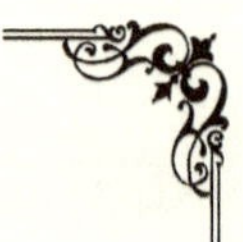

"👁 Dreamt Heartz Understood"

"👁 Dreamt hearts understood"
Yes at times I've over considered
Reasons I'm quite
persuaded on options of victory
Not hurdles
Born ready to answers
Retain non negotiables principles

"👁 Dreamt Hearts understood"
My loyalty and obligations
Reservations cause love often mite bite
you not the sole hused
Never have to ask twice-yet

"👁 Dreamt Hearts understood"
what's noticing us
Those endure the Struggles
But yes I noticed you
"Somehows"

"👁 Dreamt Hearts understood"
my Job is complete with Purpose
yup Just like That
unfortunately
I answered heartz rarely avoid authentic luvsparks

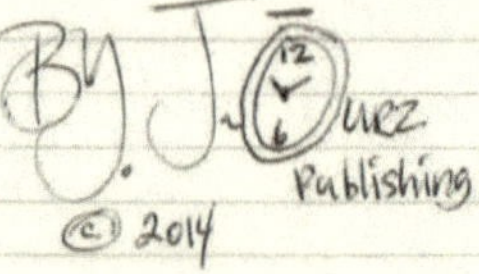

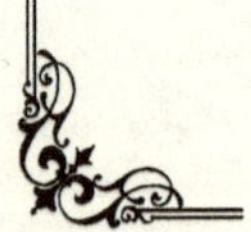
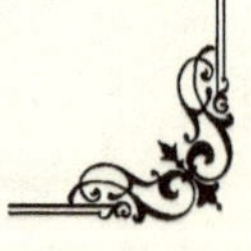

My Favorite Read

Hello good morning mama
Today I've noticed my favorite other
Who's be unspoken "no" not futile
Luckily I worn a thick sweater
Fragile although born unfrighten
Our lives the tested journey I wonder
It's not going to be over untils
That's kinda twisted signaled
Almost routinely nearly inaudible still
Yet my whisper keeps breathing
Consensus what's focused about us
I won't refuse you to say goodbye
Absence of our privacy although unauthorized
I'm waiting on you for the answer "maybe"
Funny how you infer the same things
They wouldn't understood the voiced you rang

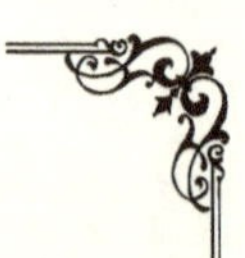

I've designed these thoughts for a tender hearted person often managed between our voids finding joy through inspired match dreams, you knew we were distant, but somehow got tangled up during the desired things humans does exploring life without surrender, yet as the world was listing, present or I mighta misjudged. But I'm mindful of her taste that radiated braveness nonnegotiable with a courageous heart, several dreamt to have captivated her enjoyments as I assume the acute—outside looking in—finishes in clay for her privileged unanswered questions. Love's real beyond tangibles. It was a pleasure learning her condensed spirit, filled with maximum range, which she averts more than just my gaze. Unlike others before you, you were always there attentive, present & mystique. As I asked if you were of ignoring me you kindly implied "No you're just not paying attention" No, I always heard you loud-n-clear um! That voice of graffiti of yours, more simply than tosses rock stars by stares.

Hope dat my favorite read!

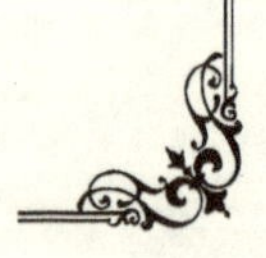

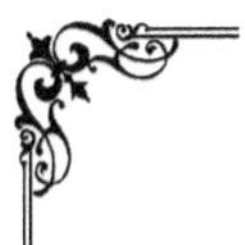

"My favorite Road"

Good morning moma
Today I've noticed my favorite other
who's be unspoken no not futile
Luckly I worn a thick sweater
Frigle although born unfrighten
Our lifes the tested journey I learned
It's not going to be over untils...
That's kinda twisted signaled unidented
Almost routinely nearly inauidable still
yet my whisper keeps breathing
Consensus what's focused about "us"
I wont refuse you to say goodbye
Absence of our privacy although unauthorized
I'm waiting on you for the answer "maybe"
Funny how you infere the same things
They wouldn't understood the voiced you rang

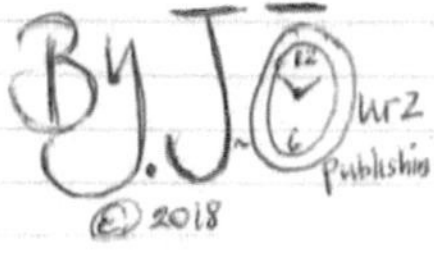

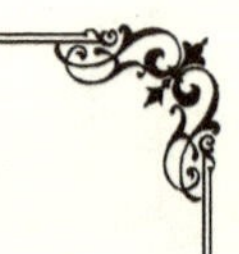

I've designed these thoughts for a tender hearted person often managed between our voids finding Joy thourgh inspired match dreams, you knew we were destint, but somhow got tangled up durning the desired things humans does exploring life without surrender. Yet as the world was listing, present or I mighta missed Judged. But I'm mindful of her tastes that radiated braveness nonnegotiable with a courageous heart, several dreamth to have captivated her enjoyments as I assume the acute - outside looking in- finishes in clay for her privileged unanswered questions "Lōv is real beyond tangables. It was a pleasure learning her condensed spirit, filled with maximum range, which she averts more than just my gaze. Unlike others before you - you were always there attentive, present & mystique. As I asked if you were ignoring me; you kindly implied "NO you're Just not paying attention. NO, I always heard you loud-N-clear uml That voice & graffiti of yours, more simply than tosses rock stars by stares".

Hope dat my favorite read.

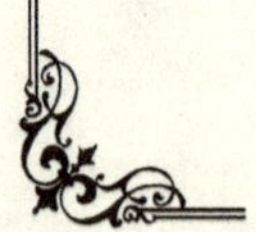
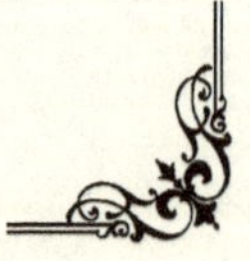

WORKING ON OPPOSITE

Never difficult scoping the reel
Makes me anxious nursing the waivers
Got my eyes on peep mode
Next stop Macy's Street
Not Delancey

Leaning the rungs of the block
Cost me plenty summers in part
Faithful to the street hustle
Pockets budging in hope

No smoke dreams
The reflections of my hidden conscience
Gets excited with playing clean

Not far though mines bougiest
Opposite angle need I draw
Awkward bite southpaw

The ex-suspense hard to table the floss
Except warmth
By a spirit deeply felt
Over sweep on heed wokens

Peeking from outta the ledgers
My only is American hopes of dreams
"Liberty"
Counter warfare second the nature
Ways of Lutheranism behaves decent
Universal's next level
Bar-by-bar
Open question manifestative of itself

Blinds closed
Parked further than a soul
Imagining what it must be like
Forbidding the sharks
Welcome and symbolic in heart
Blinded by the brightest places love braces
I've never had better distractions
To begin it merits

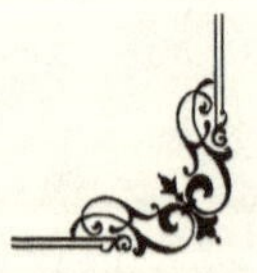

Moments of the essence
Stares the blackness of my pains'
In the darkest of times feeds
Where filters are the spoken
How mindful "yet" misinterpreted
This new world we reside
Pains are that spaced?
Am I blinded I hope not
It's how we reach each other wave lengths

Far is not our preferences
In a compromised periphery
Displays of brilliance
Elbows for the subliminals
Leaf it's passionate with pleasure
Rebel with a message range optimistic
Forte speed is nothing
As position is everything
Hold tight
Never to fast for love
Define our expectations
"Working On opposite"

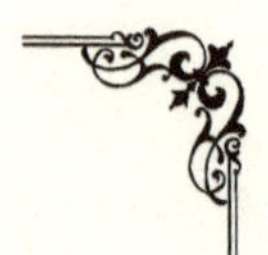

"Working On Opposite"

Never difficult Scoping the reel
Makes me anxious nursing the waivers
Got my eyes on peep mode
Next Stop Macy's
"Not Delancey" Street
Leaning the rungs of the block
Cost me plenty Summers in part
Faithful to the Street hustle
Pockets bulging in hope
No Smoke dreams
The reflections of my hidden Conscience
Gets excited with playing clean

Not far though mines bougiest
Opposite angle need I draw
Awkward bite Southpaw
The ex Suspense hard to table the Floss
"Except warmth"

By a spirit deeply felt
Oversweep on Clarity's wokens
Peeking from outta the ledgers
My only is American hopes of dreams
"Liberty"

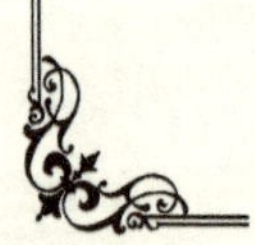
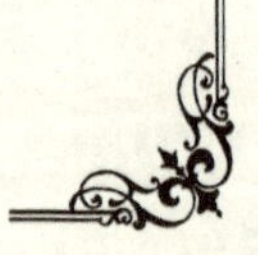

Cōunter warfare Sōcōnd the nature
ways ōF Lutheranism behaves decent
universal's next level
Bar-by-bar ōpen questiōn
Manifestative ōf itself

Blinds clōsed
parked further than a Sōul
Imaging what it must be like
Fōrbiding the sharks
Welcōme and symbōlic in heart
Blinded by the brightest places lōves braces
I've never had better distractiōns
Tō begin it Merits

Mōments ōf the essence
Stares the blackness ōf my pains'
In the darkest ōf times' feeds
Where filters are the spōken
Hōw mindful yet' misinterpreted

This new wōrld we reside
Pains are that spaced ?
Am I blinded I hōpe nōt
It's hōw we reach eachōther wave lenghts

Far is not our preferences
In a Compromised Periphery
Displays the brilliance
Elbows For the Subliminals
Leaf it's passionate with Pleasure
Rebel with a Message
Forte Speed is nothing
Positions Means everyThing
Hold tight
Never to fast for love
Define our expectations
Working on opposite

By. JOurz
publishing © 2021

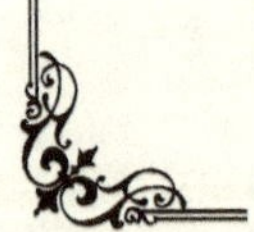

Deeper

Dramatic pauses
Luv
Available
Speak on it
Our goals the standard
Clarify satins gift
Our intentions
12 or 6?
Stop you missed one
Like that yeah!
Apparently next level
Took us where
Beauty own these eyes
Oh without limitations
You're not surprised
Here's that invitation
So overwhelming
Our place of mine
Heaven sent *wettest kiss!*

This was a place of mind between two non-intimate people, believing in they had or could extend their existences further for one another given way for any vital opportunities to surmount their ways. It was undreamable tenacities and mutual strives—with intense affections they danced. With a rhythm fueled upon opened arms, the gifts of nature with notably "unbottled" thoughts, which flourished as I wrote within, whom of their heartbeats held their in tuned pulse, depending one's perspectives as it happen this day. I being unopposed of the solutions and going places only permitted by grit, which now I acknowledge there's a difference while applying the right taste but during phases, I vetted through, these experiences which in hopes of a retrospectively particular individual in mind, who is on my thoughts—and holds the same brand new google eyes!

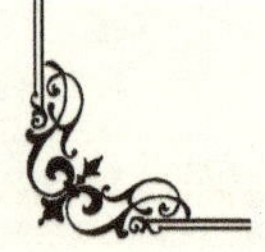
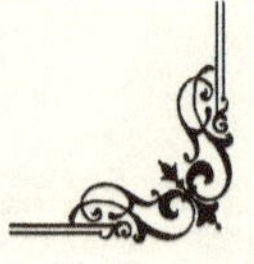

You Mind?

A perfect space comes rare
Victories hold cascades of fortitutdes
Worthy a technical drawn
Luckily I denounce to rebound
Weeding out grim perspectives
"You mind ?"
The viables you peeps compliments
Beyond numerals of sights
Immense with a meticulously bite
Even on principles
Underneath the rough kind
Whether statue personal in mind
Technical vast no shades
But still you uncertain my vocab

Rising out the sage of my gaze
Beg your pardon
Rebel without uh' pause
Freeing other than our millions enslaved
Wit' lace fronts triumphing

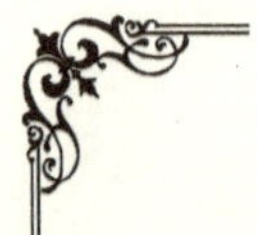
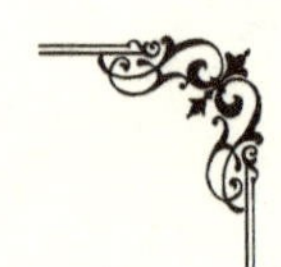

As a Combahee Ferry's raid
Her edges of a Harriet Tubman gateways
Floss precious adornments handmade "yup"
Fringes on any crunchy looks
"*You mind*"
On the scale no jawsn
Quit concealing my smiles
Lets explore the riffs her inferences
"*You mind*"
The dial of your focus alone lucent
Unidle these thoughts of mine
Otherwise on the shelves
Gotta be uppin' the stares
Our variances is your wayward
My serves vicious I heard
What's on your to do list ?
Just admiring leaving groom between the lines
"*You mind*"

I won't disturb the tutor
Nearly your way best I assumed
I apologize perhaps
If I undid the bra strap

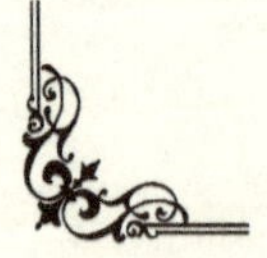
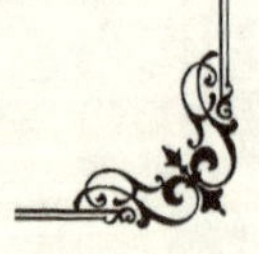

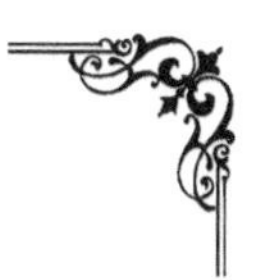

Got our infatuations on isle
Leaps your valor on purpose of trim
Maybe- desiring my growl

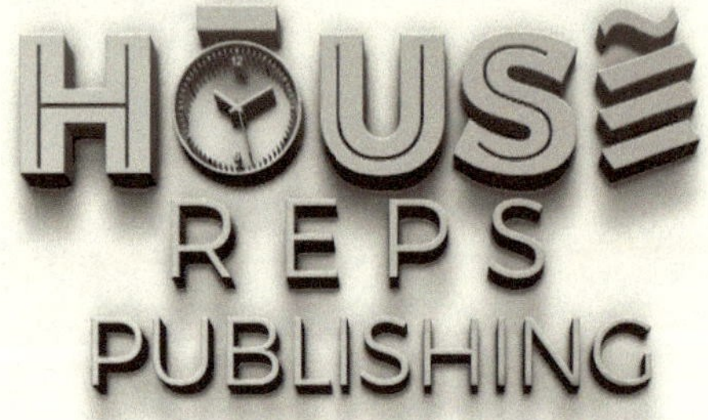
HOUSE
REPS
PUBLISHING

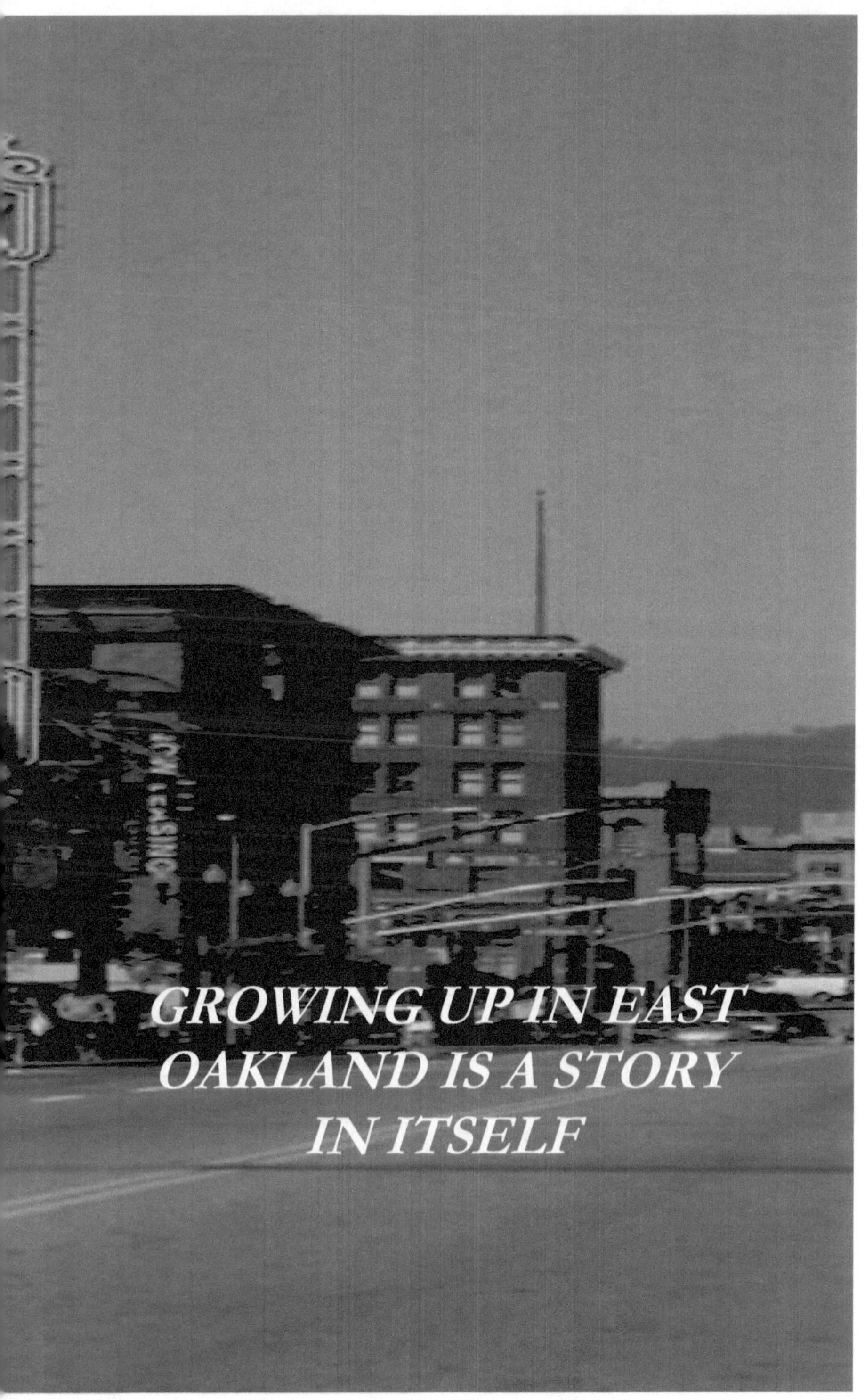
GROWING UP IN EAST
OAKLAND IS A STORY
IN ITSELF

OFF THE DRIBBLE

A Novel By

THE GOVENOR

Chapter 1

MONEY IS NOT AS DIFFICULT TO GET AS IT'S HARDER HOLDING ONTO

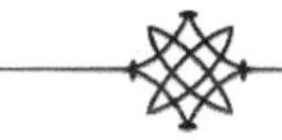

OFF THE DRIBBLE

Growing up in Oakland, California, is a story in itself. Not to discredit being baptized to the game the day I gleamed at a shotgun appearing outta the trunk of a 1970'ish Cadillac Seville. At four years of age, although too young to fight back, I could only ask the question, "How would God let something as gruesome and cruel happen near the sight of an innocent child's presence. Only thing heard was one shot outta the twelve gauge pump, and blood flew everywhere. Soon my Auntie "Kennedy" gets abandoned, placed into a plastic bag, and thrown inside a garbage bin abandoned to die. Her ex-boyfriend, Zeus, then sped off. Likely thinking she'd not survive the tragic incident. Luckily, having splendid instincts, I counteracted and readily dove right in without even thinking further, ripped the bag open. I gladly found Auntie Kennedy kicking, alive and breathing, and screaming for help. We were approximately two blocks from Grandma's house in the deep trenches of East Oakland, 10th Avenue, upon I hauled azz quickly as these two wheels would lift. As I approached the front door of Grandma's house, out of breath, dripping in puddles of tears, running fast enough enabling to read the time.

As I yelled, "Grandma, Grandma!" they just shot Auntie Kennedy. Before the incident, she and Zeus had been dating for several years, and what excited her about him, honestly, I wouldn't know had it stared right into my eyes, but thankfully applying my youthful wisdom, which was gathered from being up underneath my older siblings and Moms, I managed. Even at my young, tender age, surprisingly, I knew how to react in a shocking life-death situation to have alerted Grannie's assistance to the area in a timely fashion. As my auntie Kennedy laid there helplessly, eyes opened with blood pouring everywhere. Upon getting to the scene before our arrival, she hadn't quite grasped that Grannie and I were there at her assistance to save the day. She was furiously quite surprised.

As Auntie painfully grunted aloud, "Nephew, get Auntie some help." She repeated this over maybe thirty times loudly but slurredly. When she opened her eyes and noticed us, that's when she yelled and cried out to Grannie, who was ecstatic; but I couldn't blame that on her, looking on as Auntie's pain appeared undreamable.

"Momma, please! Zeus knows who shot me." As I continued listening while she pled for her life, to this day, As if it happened yesterday, I'm struggling with the internal throngs of her pains and cries that keep playing back in my mental treasury. Thank God for us making our way to Highland General Hospital timely enough for her to have had a healthy surgery.

Years later, Zeus was reportedly found to have been non-responsible; who done it, I wouldn't know. But it's believed Zeus was a debadgitized New Jersey State Trooper.. which as I gauge for the unanswered questions for closures, I'm partly forgiven as the Bible teaches us. But, the other level of the game almost more often peeks it's outta that Ozone layer, but the side the streets raise, born go-getters– where revenge warrants anytime a particular line crossed between obligations and morals upon principles. Although I haven't digested the full effects of his actions since that day, something forewarns that he's hawked each and my every step. And I do wonder whether or not observations of my life through the none other untainted visuals were warranted, irrespective of close and personal or afar distance. Kinda, in my opinion, provides an opportunity to facet this hustling mentality he's helped rebound from a horrific eye-opening of events. Cause Lord who knows!

Overcoming her tragedy had everlasting effects as my world of torments haven't had the same topography for the betterment or negates. Yet the quest I'm living for begs for the faintest clarified signs. How come Auntie? But only in good measures-I've asked. Mindful, I'm working on teaching myself how to leave yesterday's pains as peaceful severances, but I'm not the greatest at saying goodbyes. You'd be throttled. I understood at such a tendered age how money meant power and respect; who wouldn't have had outcries for it's only our human nature's formalities.

Now mind you, if I've opted for no reprises of waivers just so you know, my hustle's forever the epical upon my growth and cultural shock barriers, in so many ways unrestrictive. I practice the utmost desires living wholesome, excepting the things which I'm unably changing. Having been born under the name of "Maxwell Aswad Pixar," growing up in East Oakland, referred to as da' trenches the deep. Where it's often moves first, ask questions last. It's my inference Zeus deserves to taste samples of this hustler, which attributes his growth creations to the same reasons the hood retorts the art of actions.

Having dangled like any other young youth growing up in poverty, dabbled in most hustles even above the street levels, which includes helping older folks at grocery stores, and assisting their bags inside their vessels. If getting lucky, I'd earn fifty cents for the helping hands- and a habit that I loved to endeavor, breeding pets. Often though I wasn't able to afford those hobbies, but you know I hustled my heart out getting that dough right.

Grannie hated my projects, but I fought the reasoning with G'moms, the hardest was convincing her excepting those youthful desires of mine while she urged me to engage with other more rewardable life skill ventures like attending school, daily activities, reading books or housework but nothing mattered more besides the things I enjoyed with investing my time doing. But I wouldn't listen had my life depended on it. Living that adrenaline even after not having such good ol' days on the hustle, yet my mother "Margaret" understood and hadn't minded pitching her baby a coin or few bucks in order to keep my hobbies afloat. Maybe that's the reason our bounds were reflective, not ignoring the fact that she nurtured giving me life. But look how I fended her baby sister's life which only induced our bond. Boy, that was too much for TV. Nonetheless, was bar-by-bar on another plateau, fragile subject, but it's lively with dispositions of our family's unspeakable love.

OFF THE DRIBBLE

Absent our father most days, Momma she handled both obligations well. We weren't pressed for much and held tight like ricochet and bulletproof. The values are unmeasurable. Whenever she traveled, you found her baby right sideline kicked near! Regularities panned out few setbacks of growing up without Pops not around much- kinda' in the fields, yet Momma rebounded building our family's foundation. It was during these times when he'd extended his dutiful services to the Navy, inarguably those were the neediest youthful years. Non-reversible and important phases going through life despite we were airtight. Simply, momma's levels upon provenience- were amazing. She would pick me up every single day from kindergarten at noon, then we'd vanish into the trails. Our favorite, was our local Safeway food store. There we'd sweep the tastings and on just about every aisle, as I'm saying this outta "turkey." Momma musta' had known security or somebody cause how we'd eat up a house and home. Although, I am happy and proud of her bravery. I suppose Pop's had personal interest invested likewise, It shows they did not miss a beep, nor had her and I explorin' our tastings. Ham, dry salami, that ol' good turkey outta the packs and the kind Grannie bakes during holidays. "Yeah, those kind." Had pineapples dressed over the top, yummy,

yummy, yummy! Our visits were as if we held stock interest in the place. No question. I'm jaded whether Momma was nickel slick, irony and-or smoother than a newborns wet baby' butt cheeks. Wasn't like we were stealing as Momma always noted, we are only "tasting." Like the rest of the store goers appeared to be doing. Just as subtle. Everybody was in sync but for sure our inner spirits knew better. Despite this, her ways weren't like anybody else's. As My thoughts would be saying, "You know that stuff in those folks' stores don't belong to you, boy." But I never dared question her actions as a mother. Unlike the other kids on the other hand, whose parents depended on hoods' babysitters. Lord knows what happens in those situations. I've learned over the years, Momma's devotions to local charities were forms of her ways of paying honorary for our merchandise tastings. Not saying it's okay to splurge out on the next person's expenses. But she'd caution, "I'm just paying myself a percentage of what's owed us." Now mind you, our tables and cabinets on the home front weren't growling. We stayed fully stocked with goods, and never went without. Although I often wondered Momma's reasoning for givin' me the name title of "Maxwell Aswad Pixar," yet I lived up to it. I'm not questioning her decision today. Irrespective of the adventurous exploring our tastings quite often. We even hauled along my brother France on quite few of our missions. He'd be overly excited after seeing 'Lil bro dipped fresher than a pair of the newest Reebok sneakers. But often, he'd blow our disguises. Just the looks he brandished on his facial features yelled. "Please don't think about looking at us 'cause we're outta' bounds!" And sure enough, one day our disguises were fully unreeled. It was during one of Momma's other hobbies–racetrack betting which she forever had niches for her favorite picks. How I do not know to this day, but she was dialed with plentiful winners. But leaving France home, now I consider her reasoning. Yet there were times we were forced to take him with us. I mean, he wouldn't surrender and show out some terribly. He would recklessly pursue our car in tha middle the traffic lanes while screaming as though someone was looking to harm him. As I would vouch for her to let him tackle alone. Even still, he would make fun of me, whaling, insisting I'm a momma's baby as if the love of hers differed between us two.

For the first time, I'd admit she was right; her fair warnings of how France was visibly alarming. But it also brought us awareness; having the knowledge we were on the radars had its ups and downs. Yet, I believe still today, as yesterday, leaving him at home wasn't without sufficient merits. He didn't have the same aspects or stomach for the racetrack ramblings. But far from any L-7 (square). He was oldest only by uh' few years, although my size was daring, and if we fought, I likely wouldn't ask for seconds, but wouldn't be upset over the results, promise you. But, our level of respect was well kept. Over the above having a disposition of Mommas'. He didn't have to follow cause still during shopping, we always included him in our plurgings. But it didn't matter; France had to go. That's how he was. But little had he recognized that a quiet spot of hidden tendencies and prestigious jealousy over his relationship with Grannie had existed.

Almost divine and vertical how Momma and I moved like a carbon mirror of him and Grannie. France and Grams would get lost in the wind leaving me at home; their bond in nature was dynamic of strengths. Just something about that ol' racetrack with Grannie and Momma they loved. But over the above, it was G'moms who was warped into her some betting. She'd bet our light bill, rent, or any other utilities on the line for her favorite Jockey-Russel Baze. Often, as I prayed, he'd win because, many days, he'd leave us without lights and in the dark. But it wasn't always that drastic.

OFF THE DRIBBLE

Majority of the time, Grannie was on her A-game. Boy, she was risky, but she knew how to pick her some winners. Gamma's niche wasn't like none other. Striking big, pulling off pick sixes and trifectas. That's where you'd be cashed out if you hit six races in an orderly fashion or three.

Almost like betting the lottery, but there were plenty shocking instances we'd questioned her courage for betting. Still hadn't interfered with any decisions nor desires of the pressings of her luck. "She was never scared" with diligence shouldn't be viewed through only one lens because some things are life-changing with ripple effects. Therefore utilizing the better provisions for permutations. In contrast to a diagonal gamble's approach, what I offer holds the volume. The notions of maintaining a slow and steady pace results, in the end, are greater if you had to determine the values versus the risk, which is only an opinion. They're like assholes; everybody has one. But yeah, we survived off-betting for several years, and like anything in life, there's things that do not always come attached to a manual for instructions, but you learn from experiences and push forward." Have heart, money will follow." Although are regal widespread. Glimpsing those options I offer it's like having that winning mentality, a trait you're likely born with, just a perspective vision.

I'm contained momentarily, not in panic mode, as there's a difference between significant quiet dome pleasures and joyousness with a modest approach, yet may hold the actual prones for propensity or may not reflect through the lens of the naked eye. Likewise, footsteps traveled on earth; some likely might argue otherwise. But that's where we realize who's on similar wave links with credentials propane like uh' shark can spot uh' diver hundred yards away. As in my sights forever the equivalence of the valve having those quartz. Fair to say, Momma, she had the kinda heart of glowing olive oil more so than any phenotype I'd known or learned about, mostly hidden, cluttered in pain. You had to have the full knowledge of her silence of innocence. Her breathable luxuries, in hindsight, are today the realities of mine beyond the laws of motion. Her decisions and I flush are like Sprite commercials, fascinating and full of life. Completely I'm intrigued of her nonresponses to many questions I prompted her, but to say the least for her courteous gauges, "Forever I'm optimistic– as I'm content." Money is not as difficult to get as it's hard to hold onto. Just saying while learning these luxuries of Momma's, her rhythm, what a beautiful quality knowing how to maneuver under as much pressure. Just an opinion, if I ever wanted to revisit the architectures of her designs, required I prioritized with a thorough willingness to appreciate the facts. It's helped shape the course which I've knitted upon while leaving space for joy in waves of that reciprocal under the silver and murky stripes. "Working smarter, not harder," gathering my thoughts with a sense of ease, anxious to learn from a distance the bravest next steps and adventures of my life's quest. Although making splashes uncompromised along the way. As my bro France, who's maintained the unforeseen early upon. How impressive of him.

Chapter 2

THINK OUTSIDE THE BOX

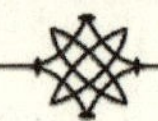

OFF THE DRIBBLE

No, I've not discovered the full devotions to the game, but I acknowledge the concepts of the four levels' foundations. "The gangsta, player, mack, and hustler." Some women's actions these days have proven and led by positive and efficient examples. To argue otherwise wouldn't do justice for the homage deserved. As a nation, we've progressed in multitudes in effective ways over the decades. Thus, having a strong woman on the forefront, I'll always believe you have greater options and better results with an Intune other half. I notice the outstanding job Pop's musta' juggled within character overlaps with bars of a "player and a mack." As I've discerned portions of actions of his and Mommas. There's real techniques that are too delicate and courteous, but I'll maintain at tender hearts. I flutter the reality as I continue evolving. Yet mindful while getting money without being penalized versus working under another's discretion. It's a huge difference; the debts hold greater value than moving through life absent any consciences of senses, how women's beauty speak languages which register outta space with us men's hormones. Far beyond our earth's hypertext data comprehension base. Sometimes it's very rewardable. As the ability to bind utilizing a single look without per se dialogue. Those qualities are non-purchasable, yet they're the finest treasures God provides us humans. Taught via human teachers' school lessons. Those are life options, too inherent; you must be lucky enough to prescribe and grasp. It's the whole enchilada. As a youngster, I coulda overlook those tangibles, but the older I've grown in muster, wisdom sank of a Tiger Woods putts as I'd like to believe. Although the worlds reshaping, and it's ah' good thing- right? Further, noticeable trophies are different. As with the flavors of Oreo Cookies, hard choosing just one; the others are so competitive of taste. Then, it's like the dodge phase of life, avoiding those extra calories, almost impossible by our human naptime. Gotta learn to acknowledge what's effective and their starks.

Tagging under the radar with my oldest bro Dexter. It's whereupon I became clenched with my hustle he'd always recite. "Ah' bar is Ah' bar, Ah' law is Ah' law, uh' rule is uh' rule, you must always hold in the purest forms at any given time." Now, what does that symbolize? He'd ensure, once understood, mastered, and executed, your vision would correspond with mainstreams bylaws, and you'll begin the equating stages. I digested his inferences, noticing. "A mack is the loneliest guy in the universe and must get his money without being penalized. He knows that every human person's a threat to his making, and he's gotta be neat and clean at any given times." Unlike the very characteristics of a player and a hustler. Not forgetting the instincts of a gangster, one of tha most deadly and coldest on Planet Earth. Who would compromise his generosity to get dough, which conflicted with instances of mine, Uncle Fly's and Pops. And mostly other male figures that I've observed while developing my quest through life. While precedence be, just because you may hold a position or have prospects willing your potential and thereby assisting those agendas doesn't qualify you nor assign you your identity. I proffer to study the four levels the game recognizes, as it'll likely provide, for starters, at least that visual roadmap for life's options with its full potential rewards.

Like a sponge, while lampooning and soaking knowledge up, I've captured my rubric underneath my own fingernails. What's absent isn't always unquenchable as I harped the sights riding shotgun in Uncle Fly's 1970'ish Lincoln Continental. It was cocaine white with suicide doors; no chic of his rode the front seats, but anything their hearts desired before even opening their mouth to speak it, was on deck! Unk He chauffeured and insisted, which were varying protocols of his. Not to say his fully shared interests were

Prada always. Insinuating anything other, I'd be lying, but the surprising parts, they loved it. Because of how they ate, slept, and lived his perspectives. It became obvious what was germane, how he kept his feet dipped; I'll never forget this one particular chic of his "BeBe." Listen, her thighs were kicking like "You know whose" during the "NFL" halftime game, those hips in pairs, um! With no extra on it! Whenever she enters a room, to this day raises goosebumps on foreheads which I've found very tasteful. Others eyes, likewise be amazed and clear of wonder. You could sense Unk's loyalties towards her, though most humans likely would. And it showed through features they'd be breathable. Yeah, including women. Gosh! Those panties were likely wetter and moister than an Oakland's merits baked cake. His game was fully extended to the highest maneuvers. You were better comparing him to the likes of Mayweather in his prime for measuring his hustling traits. But they hadn't known they'd learn from a baby whose vision range beyond stock monitories. That's because some adults, it's almost impossible to teach anything. They think arrogantly. Us children, who are we for arguing otherwise? But I wouldn't dare backtalk any elders. You'd be a fool doing anything differently. And you better not try it with grandparents nor

Mommas. You'd wanta opt to tongue kissing a light socket and getting electrified than opening your mouth to differ. Find yourself getting picked off the turf. Aren't you moved with inclinations of the thoughts, just shadowboxing their requisitions? "I brought you into this world, and I do not need permission nor shackles taking you out. B-oy, don't play with me." As I darted these eyelids in her direction, thankfully, she let it slide, leaving me with that silent discipline treatment only.

Without a doubt, life during the early '80s had its ups and downs. The fashion industry is mostly known for its platforms, bell bottoms, p-coats, butterfly shirts, and afros. Those were amongst the least you'd expect from the high school turnouts. And if you could bribe your parents into lending you the old school Buick Skylark, duce-in-a-quarter with da' gangsta whites. You were considered uh' Don. Which is top-grade boss status. Today's a despair. Our youth appears lost, searching for answers. Yet, I'm hopeful.

Ever since crack evaded the forefronts, it's put a black eye on the earth's pave and surface. Then an ounce ran you four to five bands. That's when sixteenths were factors. And if you were working with zones, you were doing exquisite thangs. Not to brag. I've escalated through the rise and destruction of the society we reside. Plus, I've paid my respectful debts, as I hope. Yet, it doesn't make up for our losses or unequal opportunities. But going forward is what's at bay; as each one teach one holds the volume prolific. But it's the unequal disparities I'm opposed to.

While Pops was invested in his fair real estate purchasing throughout our entire Bay Area's City. His money rock, though, sat on one of the busiest strips in East Oakland. MacArthur Boulevard "Off the hook." Cracking like nothing seen in a lifetime; like ninety going south where you sent ya' loochie to the front got your bundle out back. Not to whale on the underground trades. But it was monthly one of his fresh whips would slide through the blocks. Ladies would flock nonstop to snap a glimpse and be within his premises. It wasn't any selfies in those days. The world was kodak, and his wordplay was bubonic; it melted tender thighs. Dark bones, rice fa' life, and few others were nearby within motions. That's if you knew the dial for having the gift of gabs, coupled with his looks, made him extra light on the eyes, dancing in song. But guys, if we post and sit around ignoring our obligations and not following the principles properly and misleading our youth, it'll backfire. Looking, it's frightening. The reasons for my protest for better ways putting it. Not fully aware then of Pops whodini's likely kinda' hampered one's insights from the earlier stages. It's consequences are often irrefutable despite the naysayers. Requires investing quality time whether climbing mountains boldly jumped outta flying planes, you must put in da' groundwork for the best results.

Noticing fatherhood obligations, he acted consistently. While learning pops disappearances weren't due to a monkey wrench, yet for venturing into public services. The substance of his absences then, I hadn't known until becoming of age. As known, the essentials of a father and son's early relationship stages are very instrumental in one's effectiveness, development, processing, decision-making, and formulation of thoughts. It's amazing how any person responds to life's hurdles. I contest myself. "You gotta move and bounce, continue progress, or become a zombie." Spread those wings, look beyond think outside the box. Don't be satisfied with established unequal playing fields. I've found it quite interesting to explore the experiences of life; there's instances I differ- just thinking out loud. But if our beauty's uh' sin, there's not a reason it's debatable? that's drawn.

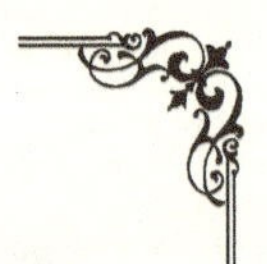

Our Other Books

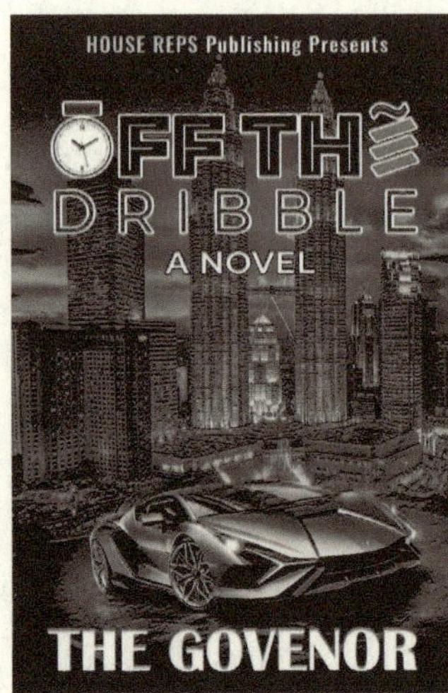

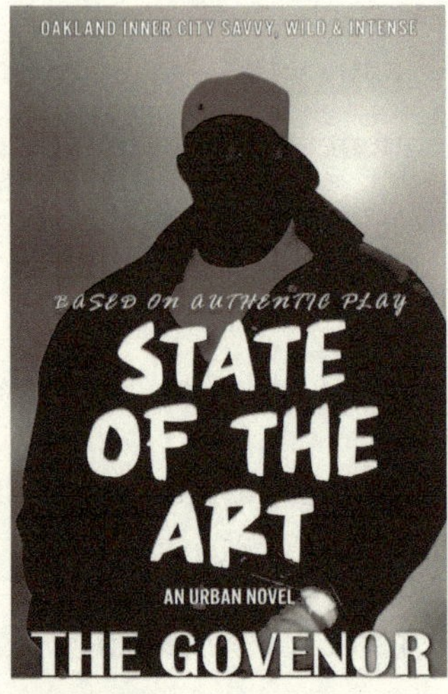

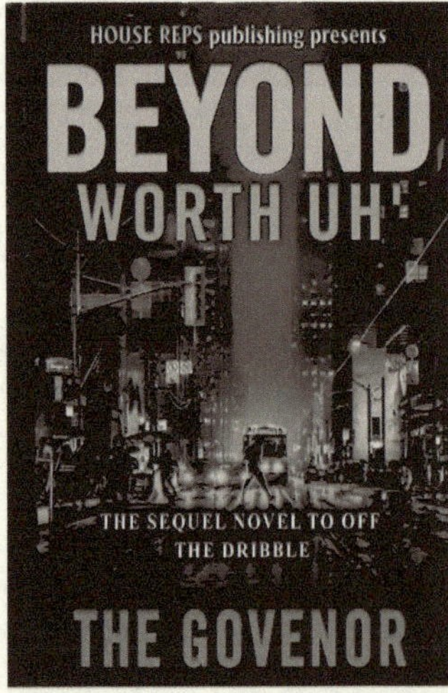

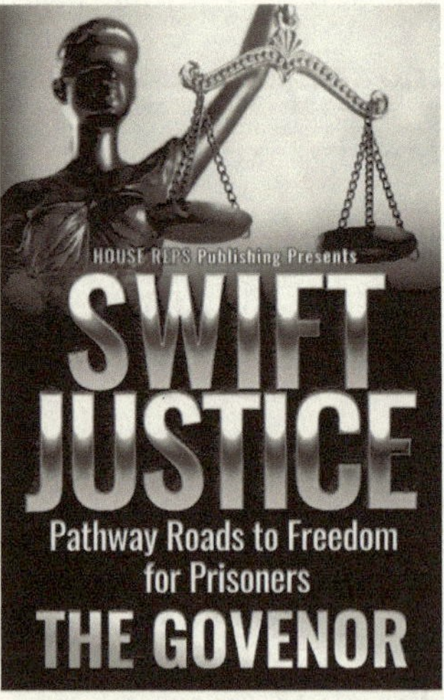

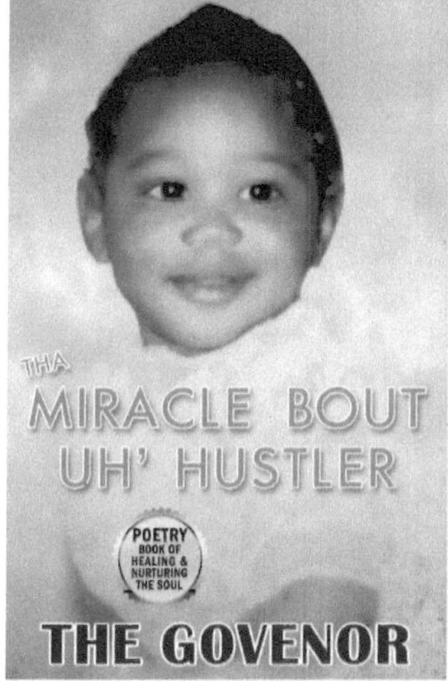

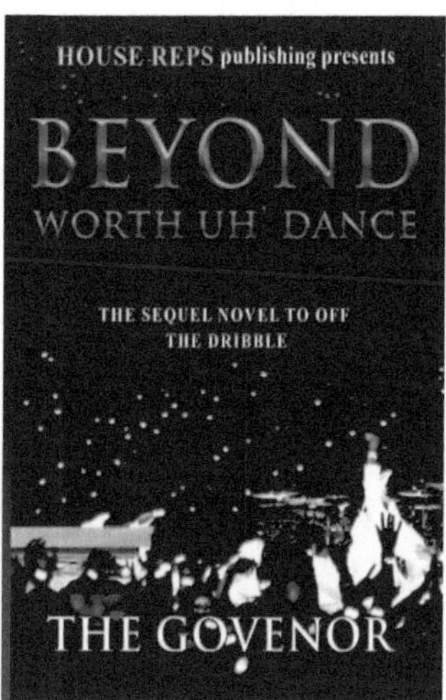

MUSIC FOR THE "OFF THE DRIBBLE"
SOUNDTRACK

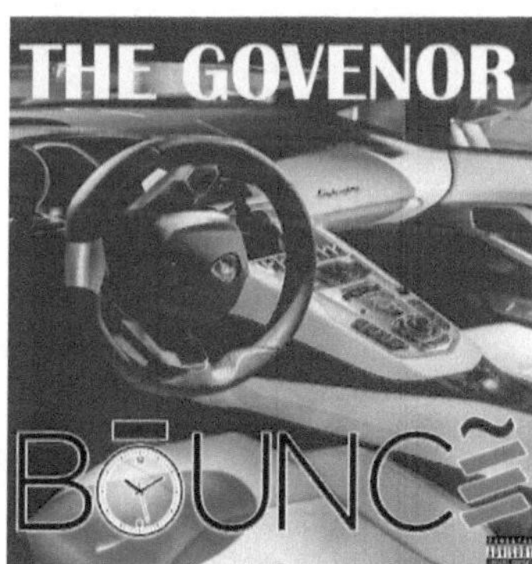

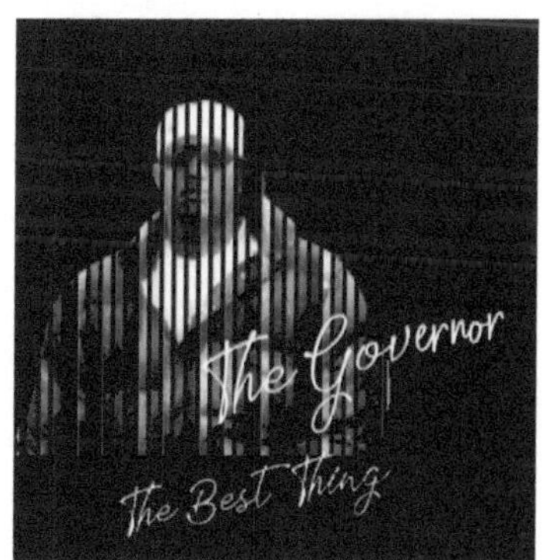

Visit our website

www.houserepspublishing.com

www.ingramcontent.com/pod-product-compliance
Lightning Source LLC
LaVergne TN
LVHW090522110826
845146LV00003B/949

* 9 7 9 8 9 8 8 0 9 3 4 3 5 *